Experiential Learning in Architectural Education

This book is designed to be of interest to many different audiences due to its cross-sectoral and transdisciplinary content. It will appeal to those within architectural higher education as well as to spatial practitioners, students, civic and governmental organizations engaged in socio-spatial projects.

The book is (1) an academic source of critical and practice-driven knowledge on experiential architectural design learning, (2) provides methods for other ways of learning in the form of design-build and live projects and (3) offers design inspiration for community-engaged spatial practices relevant to both educators and practising architects and designers.

Burak Pak is Professor of Architectural Collaborative Design, Collective Spaces and Digital Media at KU Leuven Faculty of Architecture. He holds a PhD from ITU Faculty of Architecture. After working at Carnegie Mellon University School of Architecture and Texas A&M University VIZLab as Visiting Scholar, he worked as post-doctoral research fellow at KU Leuven Faculty of Architecture on 'Alternative Urban Projects for the Brussels Capital Region'. He is co-founder of the Altering Practices (Alt_Shift) Research Group. Burak is currently teaching design studio courses and running several international and national research projects. Burak's research covers an interdisciplinary area between architecture and urban design, participation and digital spatial media. The two main and complementary focus points are exploring and enabling bottom-up participation {in} and {through} reflexive research and design practices. His research focuses on enabling inclusion in and through design. Co-creation and co-design play a central role in the research projects he participates in through which he aims to integrate social design practices, education and research. Examples of the research projects he is involved in are: 'Networked Practices for Placemaking' (EC Co-create), 'Solidary Mobile Housing' (INNOVIRIS Co-create) and 'Incubators of Public Spaces' (JPI-Urban Europe).

Aurelie De Smet graduated in Architecture at the *Hogeschool voor W&K, Sint-Lucas Gent* and in Spatial Planning at the University of Ghent. After working as independent architect for several years, she was offered a grant by the Brussels-Capital Region (Innoviris) for a three-year research project on 'The Role of Temporary Use of Waiting Spaces'. This research (promoted by Prof. Kees Doevendans and Prof. Bruno De Meulder) led to a series of publications, workshops and consultancy assignments on 'temporary use', 'bottom-up urbanism' and 'tactical urban planning'. From 2014 until 2020 Aurelie worked at the Landscape Architecture Department of the Erasmus University College, where she co-founded the Centre of Expertise Tuin+. In this context, she gained considerable experience in involving landscape architecture students in practice-oriented research on 'the gardenscape'. Currently, she is working as a researcher on the 'Solidary Mobile Housing' project at the KU Leuven Faculty of Architecture and combining this with a PhD on 'Increasing Socio-spatial Resilience through Solidary Appropriation of Urban Waiting Spaces for Housing in Brussels' (promoted by Prof. Burak Pak and Prof. Yves Schoonjans). She is also a member of the Altering Practices for Urban Inclusion Research Group and is co-teaching Community-engaged Architectural Design Learning studio and elective courses at the faculty.

Routledge Focus on Design Pedagogy
Series Editor: Graham Cairns

The Routledge Focus on Design Pedagogy series provides the reader with the latest scholarship for instructors who educate designers. The series publishes research from across the globe and covers areas as diverse as beginning design and foundational design, architecture, product design, interior design, fashion design, landscape architecture, urban design, and architectural conservation and historic preservation. By making these studies available to the worldwide academic community, the series aims to promote quality design education.

Fluid Space and Transformational Learning
Kyriaki Tsoukala

Progressive Studio Pedagogy
Examples from Architecture and Allied Design Fields
Edited by Charlie Smith

Emerging Practices in Architectural Pedagogy
Accommodating an Uncertain Future
Edited by Laura Sanderson and Sally Stone

Experimental Learning in Architectural Education
Design-build and Live Projects
Edited by Burak Pak and Aurelie De Smet

For more information about this series, please visit: https://www.routledge.com/architecture/series/RFDP

Experiential Learning in Architectural Education
Design-build and Live Projects

**Edited by
Burak Pak
Aurelie De Smet**

LONDON AND NEW YORK

First published 2023
by Routledge
4 Park Square, Milton Park, Abingdon, Oxon OX14 4RN

and by Routledge
605 Third Avenue, New York, NY 10158

Routledge is an imprint of the Taylor & Francis Group, an informa business

© 2023 selection and editorial matter, Burak Pak and Aurelie De Smet; individual chapters, the contributors

The right of Burak Pak and Aurelie De Smet to be identified as the authors of the editorial material, and of the authors for their individual chapters, has been asserted in accordance with sections 77 and 78 of the Copyright, Designs and Patents Act 1988.

All rights reserved. No part of this book may be reprinted or reproduced or utilised in any form or by any electronic, mechanical, or other means, now known or hereafter invented, including photocopying and recording, or in any information storage or retrieval system, without permission in writing from the publishers.

Trademark notice: Product or corporate names may be trademarks or registered trademarks, and are used only for identification and explanation without intent to infringe.

British Library Cataloguing-in-Publication Data
A catalogue record for this book is available from the British Library

Library of Congress Cataloging-in-Publication Data
A catalog record has been requested for this book

ISBN: 978-1-032-21291-3 (hbk)
ISBN: 978-1-032-21294-4 (pbk)
ISBN: 978-1-003-26768-3 (ebk)

DOI: 10.4324/9781003267683

Typeset in Times New Roman
by codeMantra

Contents

List of figures ix
List of contributors xi

Introduction 1
BURAK PAK AND AURELIE DE SMET

1 When Design-Build Met the Live Project – or – What Is a Live-Build Project Anyway? 9
JAMES BENEDICT BROWN AND PETER RUSSELL

2 Inspiring Public Imagination through a Micro Ecovillage for Students 25
CAMERON VAN DYKE

3 Moving from Learning to Doing: An Educational Experience of Temporary Tactical Action 43
SILVIA TEDESCO, ELENA MONTACCHINI, TOMMASO FERRARIS AND CARLOTTA GERBINO

4 Training Future Architects through Professional Responsibility: Working with Real Cases in the Master's Degree in Architecture at Vallès School of Architecture 63
MARTA SERRA-PERMANYER AND ROGER-JOAN SAUQUET LLONCH

5 Community-Engaged Architectural Design Learning as Critical Spatial Practice: The Case of the Solidary Mobile Housing Project 83
AURELIE DE SMET, BURAK PAK, YVES SCHOONJANS, SARA VANTOURNHOUT, GERALDINE BRUYNEEL, TINEKE VAN HEESVELDE, AND KEN DE COOMAN

6 Co-Creating Urban Strategies through Trans-Local Learning Alliances 105
CATALINA ORTIZ

Index 125

Figures

1.1 Project Jouberton, Klerksdorp, North West Province (2008–2010) (Photo by the authors) 10
1.2 Project Mothopong, Limpopo Province (2017–2018) (Photo by the authors) 19
1.3 Project Lesedi, Limpopo Province (2018–2019) (Photo by the authors) 19
2.1 Orbit. Future Cycles project. The Future People 2015 (Image by Cameron Van Dyke) 28
2.2 Life at Turtle Island Preserve (Photo: Cameron Van Dyke) 30
2.3 Students build wood storage racks (Photo: Cameron Van Dyke) 31
2.4 Sustainable Technology students fabricate a solar photovoltaic system (Photo: Cameron Van Dyke) 32
2.5 Freshly completed student dwelling (Photo: Cameron Van Dyke) 33
2.6 Josh inside student dwelling #2 (Photo: Cameron Van Dyke) 38
2.7 Outdoor area Jake and I built for student dwelling #2 (Photo: Cameron Van Dyke) 38
3.1 AUT's students sitting on Tablò, the structure realized during the first workshop (Photo by the authors) 47
3.2 The construction phases of the structure (Image by the authors) 53
3.3 The construction site's activities (Photo by the authors) 54
3.4 Before… (Photo by the authors) 56
3.5 … and after (Photo by the authors) 57
4.1 Participatory design workshop between students and citizens, Cardona, 2018 (Photo: Marta Serra-Permanyer) 69

4.2 "Artisan cheese factory and kindergarten" project, by Aina Santanach and Meri Mensa, Sant Bartomeu del Grau, 2016–2017 (Photo: Aina Santanach and Meri Mensa) 70
4.3 "Mas Vilanova" built project, by Iñigo Ocamica and Iñigo Tudanca, Sant Bartomeu del Grau, 2016–2017 (Photo: Iñigo Ocamica and Iñigo Tudanca) 72
4.4 "Oasis" built project, by Álvaro Alcázar, Roser Garcia, Eduard Llargués and Sergio Sangalli, Sallent, 2018–2019 (Photo: Álvaro Alcázar del Águila) 74
4.5 Medieval old town of Cardona, 2018 (Photo: Marta Serra-Permanyer) 76
5.1 SMH Participatory Action Research Cycles 2017–2019 (Image by the authors) 85
5.2 Impressions of the SMH co-creation process (Photos by the authors) 86
5.3 Schematic representation of the SMH/M (Image by the authors) 87
5.4 Configuration of the SMH project in Jette, Brussels, Belgium (Image by the authors) 87
5.5 The CEADL-framework, extending the Service-learning Model (Image by the authors) 91
5.6 The SMH modular elements (multifunctional unit – technical unit – wall panels) and examples of possible architectural configurations using those (Images by the authors) 96
6.1 Moravia Resist is the motto for the right to stay put (Photo: Catalina Ortiz) 109
6.2 Affective interactions in the digital co-design process (Source: Atlas of Living Heritage, drawn by Naiara Yumiko) 114
6.3 A re-imagined Moravia for the Atlas of Living Heritage (Source: Atlas of Living Heritage, drawn by Miguel Mesa) 117

Contributors

James Benedict Brown is Associate Professor of Architecture at Umeå University in Sweden. His PhD, *A Critique of the Live Project* (2012), provides a critical and pedagogical model for live projects in architecture education. Since 2018, he has been a guest tutor at the University of Nottingham Design/Build Studio.

Geraldine Bruyneel works for Samenlevingsopbouw Brussel, an NPO that focuses on empowering of vulnerable groups whilst working on fundamental rights, amongst others the right to decent housing. Geraldine's main interest lies in helping to build innovative solutions to socially relevant problems by combining know-how from different fields and sharing the knowledge built through these projects. Currently, she is taking up the role of project coordinator of the Solidary Mobile Housing project.

Ken De Cooman is co-founder of BC Architects & Studies, and BC Materials. As a hybrid office, BC is manoeuvring the boundaries of architecture, research, expertise and experiment, and material production and contract in all these disciplines in a doers manner. Ken's main research areas are bio-based circular materials, infrastructure as architecture, process-based design, transitional practice and start-up, local materials, contemporary vernacular architecture and de/re/post/colonialism.

Tommaso Ferraris, Architect, is co-founder and coordinator of AUT, a student team at Politecnico di Torino that investigates DIY architecture in public spaces by organizing lectures and didactical workshops with international professionals and local stakeholders. He specializes in wooden structures, made with both modern and traditional techniques.

Carlotta Gerbino, Architect, is co-founder and coordinator of AUT, a student team at Politecnico di Torino that investigates DIY architecture in public spaces by organizing lectures and workshops with international professionals and local stakeholders. She collaborates with an architectural firm in Turin and works on residential projects and interior design.

Elena Montacchini, Architect and PhD, is Associate Professor at the Department of Architecture and Design of Politecnico di Torino (Italy). She conducts teaching and research mainly on issues related to environmental sustainability, the rational use of resources and the health and well-being of users.

Catalina Ortiz is a Colombian urbanist. She uses critical pedagogies and decolonial methodologies to study the politics of space production in global south cities to forge spatial justice. She works as Associate Professor and co-Programme Leader of the MSc Building and Urban Design in Development at University College London.

Peter Russell is Assistant Professor at the University of Nottingham's Department of Architecture and Built Environment, and director of the Design/Build Studio, a vertical studio unit that delivers design-build projects in the Limpopo South Africa. He has over ten years of experience leading local and trans-national design-build projects.

Roger-Joan Sauquet Llonch is Associate Professor in the Department of Architectural Design at the Vallès School of Architecture, Polytechnic University of Catalonia. As a member of HABITAR research group, he is a specialist in rehabilitation and reuse, sustainable tourism architecture and the relation between nature and the city.

Yves Schoonjans is Full Professor in architectural history and theory and Department Chair of the Department of Architecture of the University of Leuven, Belgium. Yves' research is structured in two lines (1) Practices and discourses in a recent and contemporary context – relation between theory and practices; and (2) Everyday local identity, appropriation and urban development. In 2013 together with Kris Scheerlinck, he initiated the 'Urban Projects, Collective Spaces & Local Identities' research group, which co-initiated the Solidary Mobile Housing Project.

Marta Serra-Permanyer is Serra-Húnter Fellow and tenure-eligible lecturer in the Department of Theory and History of Architecture

Contributors xiii

at the Vallès School of Architecture, Polytechnic University of Catalonia. Within the research group Architecture, City and Culture her research specializes in autonomy of the user, participatory design and public space.

Silvia Tedesco, Architect and PhD, is Researcher in the Department of Architecture and Design at Politecnico di Torino (Italy). She carries out research and teaching activities mainly in the field of experimentation and prototyping of circular products for architecture, integration of Nature-Based Solutions in projects and outdoor comfort in urban spaces.

Cameron Van Dyke is Assistant Professor of product and furniture design at Appalachian State University in the mountains of North Carolina. He is passionate about creating positive social change, sustainability, downshifted living and intentional community. If you would like to learn more about his work, please visit: www.thefuturepeople.us.

Tineke Van Heesvelde works as a community worker for the NPO Samenlevingsopbouw Brussel. She started working with home- and houseless people from 2002 onwards. Based on her professional experiences in this context, she co-initiated the SMH project. Tineke is convinced of the participatory approach; she is convinced that solutions worked out in cooperation with a disadvantaged group are often more sustainable.

Sara Vantournhout is the coordinator of Service-learning KU Leuven, an academic program that facilitates university courses that incorporate community engagement and critical reflection in students' learning experience and process. Together with her team, Sara co-developed and facilitates more than 30 service-learning courses that involve community-engaged teaching, learning and/or research. Aside from her work in higher education, Sara has extensive experience in grassroots organizing for social justice, both in Belgium and in Brooklyn, NY.

Introduction

Burak Pak and Aurelie De Smet

This book covers a wide range of critical educational practices exploring *other ways* of teaching and learning architectural design. The cases presented in the following chapters demonstrate a shift in architectural education towards a practice-based, student-centred, hands-on, dialogic, and critical architectural design teaching culture situated in a wide variety of applied learning settings.[1] Experimenting with social and experiential modes of design knowledge construction within and beyond academia, the authors reinvent novel forms of spatial agencies responding to the growing complexity,[2] multiplicity,[3] liquidity,[4] and spatial injustice[5] in various socio-spatial contexts. The contributors reflect on the ways in which they constructed alternative learning environments beyond mono-disciplinary and teacher-centred classroom settings based on fictional design briefs and imaginary clients with unlimited budgets. Taking a critical stance towards the traditional understanding and practices of design education, the authors aim to equip students with novel experiences, skills, and competencies situating their creative thinking within complex, real-world contexts.[6,7,8,9]

This book demonstrates that design-build is re-emerging as an alternative and innovative form of architectural education situated at the intersection of academia and critical practice, extending design learning towards civic engagement and societal service. The Design-build and Live Projects cases covered in this book offer a plethora of approaches, strategies, methods, tools, and experiences to achieve these goals. They introduce a collaborative and inclusive turn in architectural design learning which echoes the examples from the past.

This book's contemporary design-build practices build on an extensive range of archetypes and experimental learning environments, such as the Black Mountain College in North Carolina and the Rural Studio at Auburn University. These archetypes were rooted in Deweyan progressive education approaches, also known as 'experiential education',[10,11] and Paulo Freire's theories on 'critical pedagogy'.[12] Central to the experiential education approach were the notions of continuity and interaction. According to Dewey, learning can only be effective if it comes from and leads to other experiences. Contesting the traditional view of education as a one-directional knowledge transmission process, Dewey proposed a dialogic student-teacher interaction. He re-imagined learning as a process through which the role of the educator is redefined. In parallel, Freire's 'critical pedagogy' is situated in the context of his theories on *'educação popular'*, a class-based approach aimed at overcoming social injustices and oppression by stimulating the 'freedom of thought'. Several strands of design-build follow a critical learning model echoing such pedagogies prioritising learning by doing, social service, as well as democratic governance and solidarity.

As mapped out by Brown and Russel in Chapter 1 of this volume, two different schools of thought are prevalent among the contemporary approaches to design-build: the American and British traditions of Design-Build and Live Projects. While the former pivots on the experiential and laborious acts of making and constructing, the latter is characterised by its intense focus on civic engagement, participatory design, and co-creation.

Design-build involves engaged learning processes that bridge co-designing, making, and constructing spaces. This approach to architectural learning thus aims at re-establishing *'the critical relationship between the designer and the medium: the materials of construction, the processes of forming and fabrication, and the constraints these place on the design'*.[13] As a form of experiential learning, the key elements of design-build are: (1) situated construction of knowledge integrating new and past experiences and concepts, (2) design and build activities for the application of knowledge in a real-world context, and (3) structured reflection.[14] Institutions can have various reasons for adopting this approach, such as providing construction experience, training students for professional practice, improving the design sensibilities of the students (enhancing awareness of place), strengthening collaborative skills, exploring new methods of project delivery, experimenting with novel materials and materiality, framing learning as a form of community service, and forwarding critical approaches to learning (as a critique of academia).[15]

On the other hand, the Live Project pedagogy focuses on immersing students in real-life projects and presenting them with real-time rather than fictional challenges. Thus, this approach aims to enable students to gain practice-ready experience and develop a sense of civic social engagement.

Introduction 3

Although Live Project and Design-build practices have a slightly different focus (varying from educator to educator and institution to institution), these approaches also have various commonalities. In academic publications and popular design media, these phrases are often used interchangeably or referred to using other, more generic, descriptions such as Project or Practice-based Learning, Learning-by-doing, (Community) Service-learning, and Community-engaged Learning. However, central to all these approaches is the premise that learning should be grounded in everyday actions and thus result from a social process, linking actors, actions, and situations.[16] As such, they can all be qualified as experiential learning[17] pedagogies. As a place for reflecting 'in' and 'on-action'[18,19,20] the design studio provides a suitable environment for these kinds of experiments, where students can learn experientially by designing and making their own projects in interactions with real-world contexts and users. Another essential aspect of these approaches is their emphasis on bodily actions in space which raises awareness on the transformative power of embodied versus representational space in mobilising resources and people and shaping meaningful places of everyday life. Altering the current practices,[21] they construct places where the possibility for committed struggle and caring social relations can arise, building collective agencies for change through the making of critical spaces of 'difference'[22] or 'otherwise'.[23]

The Contribution of this Book

In a global context in which novel forms of university-community-practice engagements are emerging and increasing, there is a lack of reflective and critical research on societal and spatial agencies of architectural design schools. Furthermore, it is necessary to develop perspectives going beyond the English-speaking schools, integrating joint reflections from local communities to understand better the impact of university-community engagement on local communities and the academic community.[24] This book aims to address these gaps by presenting a collection of case studies that unravel, amongst others, these different aspects of learning-by-making cases from South Africa, the United States, Italy, Spain, Belgium, and Colombia.

Through reflections by architecture/design teachers, practitioners, and students from internationally acclaimed schools, this book questions the concept of spatial agency from an educational perspective. Bridging across academic, civic, and spatial practice domains, the case studies each introduce original and hybrid forms of experiential learning such as 'Live-build-projects' and 'Community-engaged Architectural Design Learning'. As such, they reveal valuable lessons on dialogic methods and processes for collective spatial production in academic architecture education. By expanding beyond traditional disciplinary boundaries in academia, they present unique and original perspectives on spatial design education. These include a critical and practice-driven pedagogical method intermingling the design-build and live project approaches, innovative ways to address societal needs through diegetic prototyping and the creation of public imagination, a bottom-up educational experience using temporary tactical action, a framework for addressing the critical issues of professional responsibility, ethics, and reflexivity in practice-based education, the introduction of community-engaged architectural design learning as 'critical spatial practice', and an elaboration on knowledge co-production and co-design through trans-local learning alliances in times of remote teaching. As such, each chapter presents new perspectives on how designing and making spaces in real-world settings can promote other ways of learning situated beyond the confines of the traditional academy.

Introduction of the Book Chapters

Chapter 1, by James Benedict Brown and Peter Russell, is written as an exercise in collaborative writing by two architecture educators, one raised in the American tradition of design-build and the other in the British tradition of live projects. Presenting a critical theoretical reflection aiming at disentangling the key concepts of 'design-build' and 'live projects', this chapter draws on a decade of critical and practice-driven pedagogical knowledge gained in the context of The University of Nottingham's Design/Build Studio, which involves students in the construction of community projects in the Limpopo Province, in South Africa. This chapter can also be read as an extension of the introduction section, going deeper into the relevance and urgency of these two notions. The authors highlight the emergence of the hybrid concept 'live-build' and warn of the danger of conflating the intentions and interpretations of design-build and live project pedagogies. They stress that it is necessary to understand the differences between the pedagogy and the method of delivering that pedagogy.

Chapter 2, by Cameron Van Dyke, is a reflection on 'Diegetic Prototyping' through the presentation of a living experiment that involves the co-creation of a micro eco-village with students in Boone, North Carolina, USA. This chapter highlights how their living laboratory, situated off-campus and not (yet) officially integrated into the school curriculum, provides students with a fully immersive experience and

Introduction 5

how this inspires public imagination. The author, amongst others, highlights the key characteristics of this laboratory as (1) a critical stance towards curriculum design, (2) building of a sustainable learning community with citizens, (3) iterative prototyping as a structuring method, and (4) impact-oriented-learning planning (which results in the creation of three houses and corresponding infrastructure). This chapter shows how immersing students in this radical experiment and lived environment qualifies as experiential learning.

Chapter 3, by Silvia Tedesco, Elena Montacchini, Tommaso Ferraris, and Carlotta Gerbino, covers the case of a micro-architecture intervention carried out bottom-up by the student group *Autocostruzione Urbanismo Tattico* (AUT) as a part of a student funding initiative promoted by Politecnico di Torinoat the Politecnico di Torino, Italy. The authors elaborate on the role of Architecture Schools in supporting and stimulating student initiatives and highlight how this can help connect the university to professionals and communities. The value of this contribution lies, amongst others, in the insights it offers into the civic involvement of the university and its students. And in this way, the authors elucidate how the presented experiment created opportunities to improve student and community competencies.

Chapter 4, by Marta Serra-Permanyer and Roger-Joan Sauquet Llonch, presents a pedagogical model developed by the Vallès School of Architecture, located in Catalonia, Spain. Compared to the previous chapters, this case study discusses an experiential learning approach originating 'from within the curriculum'. The authors, amongst others, elaborate on the three key goals of the presented case: open process, social return, and hands-on experimentation. Thereby this chapter clearly highlights the novelty and necessity of constructing a social space open to conflict as a part of an architectural/design learning project.

Chapter 5, by Aurelie De Smet, Burak Pak, Yves Schoonjans, Sara Vantournhout, Geraldine Bruyneel, Tineke Van Heesvelde and Ken De Cooman, combines theoretical contributions with reflections from the case of the Solidary Mobile Housing project in Brussels, Belgium. In this chapter, the authors present a conceptual framework for understanding Community-engaged Architectural Design Learning (CEADL) as critical spatial practice. With this framework, the authors place CEADL at the intersection of 'participatory design', 'reflective practice', and 'living labs'. This approach is novel but also complementary to the ones presented in the previous chapters, as it involves seeing designers as 'cross-benching practitioners'.

Chapter 6, by Catalina Ortiz, illustrates the pedagogical project of the 'Overseas Partner Engagement' of the MSc on Building and Urban

Design in Development at University College London in partnership with diverse local organisations in Medellin, Colombia. This chapter elaborates on how research-based design, trans-local learning alliances, and critical pedagogy are pivotal for framing urban design as a progressive co-creative process. Like the previous chapter, this last chapter also reflects extensively on the theoretical frameworks used to ground the pedagogical approaches employed in the case. An interesting contribution is the analysis of the potentials and limitations of the collaborative remote work executed in the context of this case.

All the cases included in this volume cover stories about student-centred, evidence-based, dialogic, and critical architectural design teaching experiments situated in a wide variety of learning settings, resulting in situated knowledge production aimed at better preparing students to work in today's complex real-world context.

Bibliography

Bauman, Zygmunt. *Liquid Modernity*. Cambridge: Polity Press, 2000.
Canizaro, Vincent. "Design-build in architectural education: Motivations, practices, challenges, successes and failures". *International Journal of Architectural Research Archnet-IJAR* 6, no. 3 (2012), 20–36.
Dewey, John. *Democracy and Education: An Introduction to the Philosophy of Education*. New York: Macmillan, 1916.
Dewey, John. *Experience and Education*. New York: Macmillan, 1938.
Freire, Paulo. *Pedagogy of the Oppressed*. New York: Continuum, 1970.
Gregory, Alexis & Heiselt, April. "Reflecting on service-learning in architecture: Increasing the academic relevance of public interest design projects". In *102nd ACSA Annual Meeting Proceedings, Globalizing Architecture/Flows and Disruptions*, edited by John Stuart, Mabel Wilson (ACSA, 2014), 404–410. Accessed November 13, 2021, www.acsa-arch.org/proceedings/Annual%20Meeting%20Proceedings/ACSA.AM.102/ACSA.AM.102.46.pdf.
Harris, Harriet. *ARCHITECTURELIVE PROJECTS, Oxford School of Architecture 2010–2012*. Oxford: Oxford Brookes University, 2012.
Howaldt, Jürgen, Kaletka, Christoph, Schröder, Antonius & Zirngiebl, Marthe. *Atlas of Social Innovation – New Practices for a Better Future*. Dortmund: Sozialforschungsstelle TU Dortmund University, 2018.
Koekkoek, Anouk, Van Ham, Maarten & Kleinhans, Reinout. "Unraveling University–Community engagement: A literature review". *Journal of Higher Education Outreach and Engagement* 25, no. 1 (2021), 3–24.
Kolb, David A. *Experiential Learning: Experience as the Source of Learning and Development*. Englewood Cliffs, NJ: Prentice Hall, 1984.
Le Strat, Pascal-Nicolas. "Multiplicité interstitielle". *Multitudes* 4, no. 31 (2007), 115–121. Accessed February 5, 2009, http://www.cairn.info/revue-multitudes-2007-4-page-115.htm.

Pak, Burak. "Enabling bottom-up practices in urban and architectural design studios". *Knowledge Cultures* 5, no. 2, Art. No. 2 (2016), 84–102. Accessed March 17, 2022, doi: 10.22381/KC5220176.

Pak, Burak, De Smet, Aurelie & Schoonjans, Yves. "Solidary mobile housing live project". In *WTC Tower Teachings, Reports from One and a Half years of Nomadic Architecture Education in Brussels*, edited by Gideon Boie, Dag Boutsen, Rosa Fens, Gudrun De Maeyer, Bjorn Houttekier, Jochen Schamelhout, 122–129. Brussel: KU Leuven, Faculty of Architecture, 2019.

Petrescu, Doina. *Altering Practices: Feminist Politics and Poetics of Space*. London; New York: Routledge, 2007.

Salama, Ashraf M. *Spatial Design Education: New Directions for Pedagogy in Architecture and Beyond*. New York: Ashgate Publishing, 2015.

Soja, Edward. "The city and spatial justice". *Justice spatiale/Spatial Justice* 1, no. 1 (2009), 1–5.

Stein, David. "Situated learning in adult education". *ERIC Digest 195* (1998). Accessed November 13, 2021, https://www.niu.edu/citl/resources/guides/instructional-guide/situated-learning.shtml.

Viderman, Tihomir & Knierbein, Sabine. "Affective urbanism: Towards inclusive design praxis". *Urban Design International* 25 (2020), 53–62. Accessed November 13, 2022, https://doi.org/10.1057/s41289-019-00105-6.

Notes

1 Ashraf M. Salama, *Spatial Design Education: New Directions for Pedagogy in Architecture and Beyond* (New York: Ashgate Publishing, 2015).
2 Jürgen Howaldt, Christoph Kaletka, Antonius Schröder, Marthe Zirngiebl, *Atlas of Social Innovation – New Practices for a Better Future* (Dortmund: Sozialforschungsstelle TU Dortmund University, 2018).
3 Pascal-Nicolas Le Strat, "Multiplicité interstitielle", *Multitudes* 4, no. 31 (2007), 115–121, accessed February 5, 2009, http://www.cairn.info/revue-multitudes-2007-4-page-115.htm.
4 Zygmunt Bauman, *Liquid Modernity* (Cambridge: Polity Press, 2000).
5 Edward Soja, "The city and spatial justice", *Justice spatiale/Spatial Justice* 1, no. 1 (2009), 1–5.
6 Harriet Harris, *ARCHITECTURELIVE PROJECTS Oxford School of Architecture 2010–2012* (Oxford: Oxford Brookes University, 2012).
7 Ashraf M. Salama, *Spatial Design Education: New Directions for Pedagogy in Architecture and Beyond*.
8 Burak Pak, "Enabling bottom-up practices in urban and architectural design studios", *Knowledge Cultures* 5, no. 2, Art. No. 2, 84–102 (2016), accessed March 17, 2022, doi: 10.22381/KC5220176.
9 Burak Pak, Aurelie De Smet, Yves Schoonjans, "Solidary mobile housing live project", in *WTC Tower Teachings, Reports from One and a Half Years of Nomadic Architecture Education in Brussels*, edited by Gideon Boie, Dag Boutsen, Rosa Fens, Gudrun De Maeyer, Bjorn Houttekier, Jochen Schamelhout (Brussel: KU Leuven, Faculty of Architecture, 2019), 122–129.
10 John Dewey, *Democracy and Education: An Introduction to the Philosophy of Education* (New York: Macmillan, 1916).

11 John Dewey, *Experience and Education* (New York: Macmillan, 1938).
12 Paulo Freire, Pedagogy of the Oppressed (New York: Continuum, 1970).
13 Vincent Canizaro, "Design-build in architectural education: Motivations, practices, challenges, successes and failures", *International Journal of Architectural Research Archnet-IJAR* 6, no. 3 (2012), 20–36.
14 Donald A. Schön, *The Reflective Practitioner: How Professionals Think in Action* (New York: Basic Books, 1983).
15 Canizaro, Vincent, "Design-build in architectural education: Motivations, practices, challenges, successes and failures", *International Journal of Architectural Research Archnet-IJAR* 6, no. 3 (2012), 20–36.
16 David Stein, "Situated learning in adult education", *ERIC Digest* 195 (1998), accessed November 13, 2021, https://www.niu.edu/citl/resources/guides/instructional-guide/situated-learning.shtml.
17 David A. Kolb, *Experiential Learning: Experience as the Source of Learning and Development* (Englewood Cliffs, NJ: Prentice Hall, 1984).
18 Donald A. Schön, *The Reflective Practitioner: How Professionals Think in Action*.
19 Donald A. Schön, *Educating the Reflective Practitioner: Toward a New Design for Teaching and Learning in the Professions* (San Francisco, CA: Jossey-Bass, 1987).
20 Alexis Gregory, April Heiselt, "Reflecting on service-learning in architecture: Increasing the academic relevance of public interest design projects", in *102nd ACSA Annual Meeting Proceedings, Globalizing Architecture/Flows and Disruptions*, edited by John Stuart, Mabel Wilson (ACSA, 2014) 404–410, accessed November 13, 2021, www.acsa-arch.org/proceedings/Annual%20Meeting%20Proceedings/ACSA.AM.102/ACSA.AM.102.46.pdf.
21 Doina Petrescu, *Altering Practices: Feminist Politics and Poetics of Space* (London; New York: Routledge, 2007).
22 Tihomir Viderman, Sabine Knierbein, "Affective urbanism: Towards inclusive design praxis" *URBAN DESIGN International* 25 (2020), 53–62, accessed November 13, 2022, https://doi.org/10.1057/s41289-019-00105-6.
23 Doina Petrescu, *Altering practices: Feminist politics and poetics of space*.
24 Anouk Koekkoek, Maarten Van Ham, Reinout Kleinhans, "Unraveling University–community engagement: A literature review", *Journal of Higher Education Outreach and Engagement* 25, no. 1 (2021), 3–24.

1 When Design-Build Met the Live Project – or – What Is a Live-Build Project Anyway?

James Benedict Brown and Peter Russell

Introduction

Since 2009, the Design/Build Studio in the Department of Architecture and Built Environment at the University of Nottingham (UoN) in England has engaged more than 350 students of architecture in the design and construction of crèches in South Africa. Over a period of more than ten years, our students have raised more than half a million pounds to fund the construction and delivery of childcare facilities that meet the accreditation requirements of federally supported childcare vouchers. At the time of writing, we estimate that more than 2,000 South African children have attended a crèche built by the studio.

UoN builds these crèches with the collaboration of two non-governmental organisations (NGOs): first, Education Africa and, more recently, the Thušanang Trust. Education Africa is a non-profit organisation founded in 1992, based in Johannesburg, South Africa, the work of which is broadly focused on poverty alleviation through education. Thušanang Trust is a more geographically focused non-profit organisation founded in 1986, established as a charitable trust in 1992, and based in Haenertsburg, Limpopo Province, concerned with the development and well-being of young children, largely through the development of community-based Early Childhood Development (ECD) centres. Having established a relationship with Education Africa first, since 2014 the Design/Build Studio has worked exclusively with the Thušanang Trust on the construction of accredited ECD in Limpopo Province.

The UoN Design/Build Studio is rooted in the idea that the study of architecture is inherently about buildings, and that through the experiential act of building we can all (both teachers and students) become better designers. The studio offers a comprehensive project-based learning experience with a tangible impact on students and

DOI: 10.4324/9781003267683-2

partners in the communities in which it works. The studio is an exception in the UK: an unusual hybrid of the North American tradition of design-build and the British tradition of the live project. Given recent developments in the literature exploring these two traditions, this chapter takes the opportunity to present ten years' worth of critical and practice-driven pedagogical knowledge and to inspire other teachers and students to learn from our mistakes and better shape their initiatives.

A Critical History of the UoN Design/Build Studio

In the academic year 2008/2009, a large multidisciplinary project drew teachers and students from across the Department of Architecture and Built Environment at UoN to design and build a crèche in the community of Jouberton in Klerksdorp, North West Province, west of Johannesburg, South Africa (Figure 1.1). The project was widely published and recognised for its innovation, although as an endeavour was at the limits of the capacity of the department to be able to repeat sustainably. After an interlude, however, the Design/Build Studio

Figure 1.1 Project Jouberton, Klerksdorp, North West Province (2008–2010)
Photo by the authors.

returned to South Africa in 2011 to undertake its first project in Limpopo Province, in the far north of the country.

The early projects unfolded in a pattern that is familiar to many long-standing design-build studios: an initial one-off initiative was undertaken in Jouberton without any intention to be repeated and with a largely uncontrolled commitment of time and effort. In hindsight, we can recognise that the ambition of these early projects was beyond the scope of what was realistically possible, demanding more time and effort than forecast to be completed. Given the overseas location of the projects, many students and prospective students who were not involved in these projects discovered and engaged in them via imagery disseminated to promote the studio, department, and University. This presented a conundrum because as the (increasingly corporatised) University marketed the outcomes of our international design-build projects to prospective students, they rightly began to expect that such an opportunity would also be available to them during their studies. Thus began the second distinctive phase in the history of the studio, in which the department began to offer semi-regular projects as part of the curriculum but without a clear commitment to a longer-term plan.

This emergent phase of the studio predates the use of the "Design/Build Studio" moniker at UoN. Each project was named in a somewhat arbitrary fashion by students picking a name from a Sotho dictionary before departure from the UK. While this reflected one aspect of the university's student-focused approach, allowing students to choose a name for the project was precisely the kind of colonial act of appropriation that we work to avoid since it effectively denied that the crèches and communities in which they were located already had names. A strong focus on the student experience contributed to the emergence of an identifiable design-build studio, one that was offered as an elective pathway through the design courses alongside other thematic or conceptual studio units offered by other teachers. The studio became defined by the recognition that the consequence of students' design decisions would be played out in real-time on a building project, which a normative design studio could not replicate. Students were encouraged to experiment and use the invitation to build as an open door for learning through the testing of ideas. The University managed to take this approach for several years, and it is a testament to the dedication and skill of the staff involved in this period that they managed to achieve a level of stability, despite only year-to-year support.

During the 2017/2018 academic year, the University began to shift from a series of one-off projects with no connection between them to a more cumulative approach with a singular pedagogical ethos: one that placed utmost importance on a more refined acknowledgement of responsibility towards the clients and communities which we were working. The change in naming practice was perhaps the most visible acknowledgement of this shift: we were not going to South Africa to indulge our students' whimsy; rather we were going there to deliver a building according to the needs and aspirations of our clients.

In 2019, for the first time, a dedicated research visit to all buildings previously completed by the studio was used to shift the focus of the studio from exclusively design-build to also consider the social impacts of the endeavour. From this point forward, we intentionally adopted an approach that required us to take a back seat in the decision-making process, trusting earnestly our NGO partners and the headteachers with whom we worked. They provided the local and subject-specific expertise required to make crèche facilities that were – perhaps – architecturally more conservative but more functional and nuanced in their spatial composition. This is not an insignificant learning task we now set for our second-year undergraduate students, who come from a highly normative first-year design studio environment.

In the 2018/2019 academic year, this approach culminated in the agreement to take on our largest building to date, a crèche measuring 500m^2 and serving the largest number of children yet. Experience suggested that such a scale might be beyond our capability. We discussed this at length and came to the conclusion that having been given this opportunity, it was not our place to build something that didn't meet the spatial requirements set out by the client or the local governance. We were faced with the choice of either designing something that was fit for purpose (i.e. large enough to accommodate the demand for childcare in the community) or to walk away altogether. This is where the studio finds itself now: in a place to confidently look to the future and identify a longer-term action plan with a commitment to the community that hosts us.

Disentangling Design-Build and Live Projects

As two teachers from two countries that Bernard Shaw said were separated by a common language, we quickly identified a problematic confusion in some of the literature. One of us was raised in the American tradition of *design-build* (Russell) and one in the British tradition of *live projects* (Brown). *Design-build* projects are characterised by a rich engagement in the manual labour of architectural construction, whereas live projects are characterised by a focus on the soft skills of architectural design: consultation, communication, and negotiation with real clients about real projects. In contemporary literature in our field, we identified a problematic conflation and possible confusion of these terms. Reviewing the literature of projects published by students and educators over recent years, we see a new term gaining currency in pedagogical discourse: that of the *live-build*.[1,2,3,4] Chad Kraus alludes to how *design-build* can be appended to *a live project* but is there more to this conflation of terminology?[5] While the idea of a "live-build" is less common than either "live project" or "design-build," its emergence prompts us to question what might be the implication of this apparent merging of these related but distinct American and British traditions. To further clarify this matter, we argue that a design-build studio addresses the separation inherent in normative architecture education, namely, that students acquire the knowledge and skills of designing buildings separately from those of constructing them. The professionalisation of our discipline is one that took place slowly and involved the gradual replacement of training through apprenticeship with education through university studies. Design-build teaching in American architecture education emerged from a 1960s social, political, and educational environment – one in which the perceived elitism of architects and universities was being challenged. At the outset of the longest-lasting design-build project at the Yale School of Architecture, Dean Charles Moore set out the goals of teaching social responsibility and demystifying the construction process for students.[6] Kraus writes that design-build education "addresses a knowledge gap within contemporary architectural pedagogy and contributes to building a better bridge between the academy and the profession."

A live project emerges from similar sentiments as design-build but manifests itself in different ways. Rachel Sara, who wrote the first doctorate to explore the live project in architectural education, writes that a live project is "a type of design project that is distinct from a typical studio project in its engagement of real clients and user, in real-time settings." Jane Anderson and Colin Priest, who facilitate the publication of exemplar projects through a dedicated web archive and portal, write that "a live project comprises the negotiation of a brief, timescale, budget and product between an educational organisation and an external collaborator for their mutual benefit."[7]

A historical survey undertaken as part of one of our PhD dissertations, which developed a pedagogical critique of the live project in British and Irish architectural education, found the first live projects at the Birmingham School of Architecture in the 1950s, where students were involved in the design and construction of several small public buildings.[8] These experiments in construction, while lying closer to the American design-build model, remained an anomaly that survived only for as long as the tenure of the charismatic head of the Birmingham School, Douglas Jones from 1947 to 1962. Live projects re-emerged in number in British architecture education in the 1990s, but their focus had shifted from a critique of architectural production to the promotion of the social responsibility of the architect.

Referring to Anderson and Priest's definition, Kraus addresses the convergence but also a divergence between design-build and live projects.

> The architectural live project is a form of experiential learning in the architectural academy ... The term live project, then, is not a synonym for designbuild [sic] but rather an umbrella. The US context lacks a universally accepted term for architectural projects that engage constituencies beyond the architecture studio but that are not designbuild-based (which may explain why these two terms have been erroneously conflated).[9]

Our interpretation is that design-build projects are a response to the perceived divide between the acts of designing and building buildings. Live projects are, instead, a response to the lack of engagement with real clients, briefs, timescales, budgets, and end-products in normative architecture education.

Confusing Design-Build and Live Projects

The Design/Build Studio at the UoN is unique in British architectural education for several reasons. Most importantly, it is the closest and longest-lasting example of a design-build programme in the North American tradition in any British university. Many comparable institutions in the UK have undertaken design-build projects in their studios, but none has returned to work with the same client so many times, nor established such a lasting and mutually beneficial relationship as that between the UoN and the Thušanang Trust.

There are other examples of similar but different endeavours in British universities. The Architectural Association's (AA) Hooke Park campus, about 200km southwest of London, provides the AA with a platform for hands-on teaching and research in the design-build tradition, principally via a dedicated MArch/MSc programme called Design + Make. Hooke Park is a good example of a sustained endeavour in architectural education that engage students with teaching and research through design-build, notably in the construction of various buildings on the 142-hectare campus itself. However, without an external client or community that students serve, the projects at Hooke Park remain oriented around an exploration of the materiality, structure, and technology of making buildings.

Where live projects become established in schools of architecture, project offices often follow. Project offices such as those at Leeds Beckett University and Live Works at the University of Sheffield provide an infrastructure that can translate live projects into practice. However, this is where live projects begin to morph away from an educational endeavour towards a kind of professional practice. To some extent, whereas live projects are often defined by their pursuit of a practice that is not in direct competition with architectural practice, the project office model can be understood as an attempt to re-shape the academy in the image of the professional practice of architecture. Design-build projects are often defined by the inability of their clients to procure buildings through mainstream architectural practice. Whereas project offices aim to replicate the function and procedures of architectural practice, design-build projects (and studios) tend to operate differently.

A Chance to Reflect

The coronavirus pandemic interrupted our programme of building in South Africa. The 2019/2020 project at Malahlela, Limpopo was postponed just ten days before staff were due to depart London. The pandemic prompted a concentrated effort to maintain and strengthen the partnerships and relationships on which the studio has been built. Text messages, emails, holiday cards, and the occasional video call have – we hope – kept our network in place, and at the time of writing the studio is planning to resume the project at Malahlela in the first quarter of 2022. During the pandemic, we at UoN also worked to establish relationships with new South African stakeholders, taking advantage of distance learning to finally introduce a South African perspective to our teaching. The single greatest advantage of online teaching was that we could now routinely engage with expertise in South Africa throughout the academic year, and not just during the short period on site.

Most importantly, COVID allowed all architectural educators to confront our own existential confusion about how we teach architecture, notably the design studio.[10] The studio is a complex and multi-dimensional thing: a physical space, a temporal space, a pedagogical space, and a socio-cultural space. We cannot assume that we share the same definitions of the studio, nor that we refer consistently to the same dimensions. In the panic of an enforced relocation of studio teaching from a proximate studio to a virtual one, we had an opportunity to interrogate precisely what we mean (and what we value) when we talk about design studio and architectural education. For those of us engaged in the Design/Build Studio at UoN, we faced a renewed opportunity to respond to perennial questions about our studio and its pedagogy. First and foremost, given the immediately apparent positive effect that the COVID-19 pandemic has had on global air pollution,[11] why do we persist with an endeavour that involves an 18,000km round trip for every student? Given how the *Rhodes Must Fall* campaign has exposed the persistent legacy of colonial structures in African universities. Why, when the links between poverty and diminished ECD and opportunity are just as apparent in the UK,[12] aren't we building childcare facilities in Nottingham? While our projects have been paused, it has been important to give serious consideration to the question: why do we persist in building in South Africa? The financial, environmental, and social impacts of moving sixty staff and students 9,000 km each way are not insignificant. The degree to which such a collective effort might benefit less privileged communities on our doorstep is not to be under-estimated. Well before COVID-19, the Design/Build Studio had already started to identify potential partners for projects in the vicinity of Nottingham. Having rendered international travel impossible, COVID-19 allowed the UoN Design/Build Studio to accelerate these plans, and for the first time we undertook a building project in the UK. In 2019, in parallel with designing a project for South Africa, the studio designed a small teaching space for an educational charity in Nottingham, and we were able to undertake the construction of this project in the spring of 2021, during the first significant easing of restrictions in the UK. Undertaking a project in the UK taught us a great deal about the attitudes and expectations of our students. Surveying our students, we found that they valued the opportunity to build in South Africa more than the build in the UK, preferring South Africa over the UK at a ratio of 8:1. Student surveys revealed that building closer to campus was not perceived to have generated the same quality of learning as building internationally. Student feedback revealed how it was considered to be a lesser experience, just another class that co-exists with on-campus teaching instead of being an immersive experience. The day-to-day realities of managing continued study just a few miles away from the site reinforced their perception of this being a lesser experience. Having one foot in their normal place of residence and study meant that students suffered from the obligation to manage their own logistics, transport, and catering. Both staff and students struggled to manage other professional obligations, such as family, which are normally more clearly demarcated when students travel far overseas. In short, the local project was no one's first love.

We also discovered that undertaking a design-build project closer to home attracted an uneven amount of institutional scrutiny. That is not to say that we were exposed to more scrutiny, in fact, the local project probably attracted less scrutiny from our colleagues in other departments, but it was decidedly uneven. International travel attracts a sense of urgency and a useful collective understanding of finality when the plane leaves. Undertaking a design-build project internationally forces us to be as prepared as we possibly can be. Furthermore, staff time is decidedly unequal when working closer to home. The UoN Design/Build Studio relies on staff (both teachers and technicians) to volunteer their time. In exchange for this, we provide 100 per cent of all expenses, including travel, accommodation, sustenance, and the experience of a trip to South Africa, albeit one which is spent almost entirely on-site. When we work locally to the campus this isn't possible, yet staff continue to work for free, encountering additional costs with limited support from the University. A further and previously underappreciated value of an international design-build project is the productive blurring of the staff-student boundary. We begin by undertaking a major international journey together, embarking on a three-hour transfer to an airport, with all the frustrations and inconveniences that follow, a 12-hour overnight flight and another eight-hour bus transfer: and that is just on day one. For the following fortnight, students and staff live together: we eat together, we work together and we solve problems together: all day, every day. It can be very unfamiliar for students and staff – but in this familial setting, there is an opportunity for bonding that is unrivalled in the UK university experience. This is wholly absent in a build that is close enough to campus for us all to go home and sleep in our own beds again.

The forced intermission of the COVID-19 pandemic has given us an important opportunity to reflect on the value of dislocation in design-build projects and, more broadly, the very great value of study abroad to both students and teachers. The experience of removal from one culture and the often-jarring relocation to another opens the door for new perspectives and reflection on one's background, education, and the privilege it may bring with it. It is at this moment that the UoN Design/Build Studio values above all others: the genuine and collective understanding of inequality and our role in it. This perspective allows us to become not only better designers but also better citizens, and to work in the future to begin to address some of the inequality we see. We do not want to be graduating architects who will design housing schemes with poor doors. Dislocation means that "assumptions of what constitutes 'good' design are significantly challenged – instead of relying on a formal move, a unique form, or a provocative concept, the design [...has...] to rely on the structuring of space, accessibility, functionality, buildability and detailing."[13] Undertaking such a project outside our comfort zone heightens the opportunity for these discoveries: in the words of John Culkin, "we don't know who it was discovered water, but we're pretty sure it wasn't a fish."

Beyond the pedagogical benefit of dislocation, there is a widely held understanding that studying abroad is a net positive for students. Simple metrics of employability, assessment and degree classification bear this out – as do post-travel surveys that suggest even deeper value in the personal growth and maturity of returning students. A broader reading of the definition of study abroad (as discussed at length in Engle & Engle 2004) clearly shows that study abroad is not as simple or myopic in definition as the overzealous pursuit of the individual exchange. Shorter programmes have value as well. Programmes focused on service have value, and an in-depth service-based programme offers a unique opportunity for students to pursue this value. We travel because to not travel is to risk isolationism. Mark Twain writes:

> travel is fatal to prejudice, bigotry, and narrow-mindedness, and many of our people need it sorely on these accounts. Broad, wholesome, charitable views of men and things cannot be acquired by vegetating in one little corner of the Earth all one's lifetime.

Given the harmful environmental consequences of excessive commercial air travel, it might seem contradictory to persist with such carbon-intensive models of international design-build. However, if we are to collectively recognise our responsibility to travel less often in the interest of the environment, then we should be able to pack more personal and collective good into what little travel we do.

We also used this period to test out some of our critical reflections at academic conferences. At the *Building Beyond Borders* symposium hosted only by UHasselt in Belgium in November 2020, we presented a paper that explored what we now recognise as a motivational misalignment between our different project stakeholders, mapped out in a series of diagrams (one of which is shown in Figure 1.2).[14] A month later, for the Architecture MPS conference *Teaching-Learning-Research: Design and Environments* at the Manchester School of Architecture, we explored some of the difficulties around the intersecting definitions of design-build and live projects, which became, in turn, the progenitor of this chapter (Figure 1.3).

Figure 1.2 Project Mothopong, Limpopo Province (2017–2018)
Photo by the authors.

Figure 1.3 Project Lesedi, Limpopo Province (2018–2019)
Photo by the authors.

Exhaust All Other Possibilities First

We have come to realise the responsibility that comes with committing to work with our clients and communities on design-build projects. To paraphrase Chad Kraus (*op.cit.*), if design-build projects in architecture education set out to address a knowledge gap between pedagogy and practice, their outcomes are highly unlikely to be delivered in any other way. That is to say, if we don't undertake these projects, it is unlikely that they will ever be realised. A parallel design-build studio might emerge in a South African university, or another overseas institution might step in and develop some variation of the model that we employ: but these scenarios only serve to emphasise that if a design-build project in a school of architecture falls through, it is unlikely to be realised. In the UK, however, if we don't undertake a design-build project to deliver a building, sooner or later someone else will. The proximity of design-build endeavours in British schools of architecture to mainstream architectural practice is much closer, whereas the distance between our design-build practices and mainstream architectural practices in rural South Africa is vast.

One observation of live projects in architecture education which has proven to be insightful is the recognition that problems arise when schools of architecture start to compete with commercial architectural practice. Live projects do not replicate normative architectural practice, rather they complement it. The experiences of longer-lasting live project programmes, such as that at the University of Sheffield, have shown that students, clients, and communities all benefit from the careful and proactive management of expectations.[15] Students should not be expected to be capable of providing a service that is equal to that provided by a qualified and licensed architect. Live projects are most successful when they deliver an outcome that a practising architect could not: even more so when the outcome provides the client with a wealth of material that forms a point of departure for the client to develop a project further, and perhaps even employ an architect.

The lesson from advocates of design-build projects is less to do with the management of expectations, rather the importance of knowing when it is appropriate to build and what it is appropriate not to. We do our best work in the UoN Design/Build Studio when we are listening for answers instead of offering them. If our client tells us that the roof of their crèche should not be flat, this is a design opportunity instead of a constraint. This is the consequence of deeply embedded local knowledge, and our role is to become a tool in the hand of the client. The representatives of the Thušanang Trust know exactly what new buildings need to be built and which of our previous projects need to be renovated or reconfigured. If they could do this work now and without our participation, they would. But we will keep going back and we will keep building until there is nothing left for us to build.

Is There Such a Thing as a Live-Build?

In this chapter, we have considered the dangers of conflating the intentions and interpretations of design-build and live project pedagogies. Both are influential and important applications of the principles of experiential learning, but we believe they must be disambiguated. If we accept that design-build pedagogy is about addressing the professional knowledge gap between architectural education and practice and that live project pedagogy is about addressing the experiential gap between architectural education and practice, can we speculate that "live-build" might be a refinement or development of its two distinct progenitors? We would argue that an uncritical reading of the design-build model as a purely pedagogical approach leads to a conflation of its origins and intentions. Both design-build projects and live projects are inherently critical of the academic environments in which they operate and the professions which they serve. Yet in confusing the distinctive origins of these two traditions, we risk muddying our conceptual understanding of the respective types. Furthermore, we risk confusing pedagogy (i.e. the theory and practice of learning and teaching) with a method of delivering that pedagogy.

Why do we, at the UoN, believe so strongly in the importance of students building far away from campus as part of their architectural education? In the American tradition of design-build, we recognise that the intense nature of hands-on problem-solving experienced by constructing a building in which you had a hand designing amplifies and enriches the problem-based learning of architectural education. We also believe that the design-build approach has the potential to re-centre designers as generalists, offering a correction to decades of creeping specialisation and creation of sub-disciplinary siloes between the different skillsets required to construct buildings. Finally, we have witnessed first-hand, year after year, the value of studying abroad together. This kind of endeavour is both different from and yet complementary to the Erasmus, Erasmus+, or other international exchanges undertaken by individual students.

Our position on the differences between design-build and live projects should not be interpreted as any kind of opposition to live projects:

rather it should be interpreted as a call to renew the important epistemological and pedagogical differences between our two specialisms. These two approaches are different yet complementary. Since the design studio provides for a broad spectrum of learning and teaching, we hope that more students of architecture will get the opportunity to directly experience or indirectly observe the processes and outcomes of both live projects in the British tradition and design-build projects in the American tradition.

To that end, it is important to interrogate the subtle ways in which both live projects and design-build projects critique the normative design studio, the "signature pedagogy" of architectural education. In the UK in recent years, many schools of architecture have interpreted the ARB/RIBA validation condition of 50 per cent of the curriculum being delivered through design studio to mean that 50 per cent of a student's schedule must be designated as "studio" time. Where interpreted intelligently, the quadripartite "space" of the design studio discussed earlier can become a site of enriched synthesis, where concerns of design, structure, technology, environment, and community share equal value. All too often, however, the design studio becomes a site of lazy indulgence, where the act of designing is valorised as an activity that consumes endless hours of solitary pencil-pushing and chin-stroking. We want our graduates to have experienced and to have understood surveying, engineering, costing, finance, project management, and (of equal importance) first aid. These vital professional skills are not served with consistency in normative architecture education, and it is not enough to place the burden of delivering them through the normative design studio. Live projects and design-build projects do different things, and in so doing they both attempt in different ways to correct the weaknesses and omissions of how we have become accustomed to doing things.

Bibliography

Agapiou, Andrew & Salama, Ashraf M. "Shaping the future of architectural education in Scotland," *Charrette* 3, no. 1 (2016): 1–5. https://www.ingentaconnect.com/content/arched/char/2016/00000003/00000001/art00001.

Anderson, Jane & Priest, Colin. "Developing an inclusive definition, typological analysis and online resource for live projects," *Architecture Live Projects Pedagogy into Practice*, edited by Harriet Harriss and Lynette Widder. Abingdon: Routledge, 2014, 9–17.

Anderson, Jane & Priest, Colin. *Live Projects Network*. Accessed 1 December 2020. http://liveprojectsnetwork.org/about/.

Brown, James B. "A critique of the live project," PhD thesis. Belfast: Queen's University Belfast, 2012.

Brown, James B. "From denial to acceptance: a turning point for design studio in architecture education," *Distance Design Education.* Accessed 1 December 2020. https://distancedesigneducation.com/2020/05/11/from-denial-to-acceptance-a-turning-point-for-design-studio-in-architecture-education/.

Brown James B. & Russell, Peter. "Motivational misalignment: managing the competing drivers of trans-national design-build in rural South Africa," Paper presented at *Building beyond Borders: Reflecting on the Dynamisms of Intercultural Collaboration in Build Projects*, Hasselt University, 9–10 November 2020.

Burford, Neil and Robertson, Carol. "Prototype Zero Energy Studio: a research-led, student-centred live build project," *Brookes eJournal of Learning and Teaching* 8 (2016): 3–13.

Butterworth, Carolyn & Others. *A Handbook for Live Projects.* Sheffield: University of Sheffield, 2013.

Christiansson, Jörn, Grönvall, Erik & Yndigegn, Signe Louise. "Teaching participatory design using live projects: critical reflections and lessons learnt," *Proceedings of the 15th Participatory Design Conference* 1 (2018): 1–11.

Gautam, Sneha. "COVID-19: air pollution remains low as people stay at home," *Air Quality, Atmosphere & Health* 13 (2020): 853–857.

Hayes, Richard W. *The Yale Building Project: The First 40 Years.* New Haven, CT: Yale University Press, 2007.

Kraus, C. *Designbuild Education.* Abingdon: Taylor & Francis, 2017.

Lloyd, Eva. "Early childhood education and care: poverty and access. Perspectives from England," in *The SAGE Handbook of Early Childhood Policy*, edited by Linda Miller et al. London: SAGE, 2017, 268–286.

Schneekloth, Lynda & Shannon, Scott. "Easing boundaries through placemaking sustainable futures study abroad program," in *Service-Learning in Design and Planning: Educating at the Boundaries*, edited by Tom Angotti et al. New York: New Village Press, 2011, 171–188.

Notes

1 Andrew Agapiou & Ashraf M. Salama, "Shaping the future of architectural education in Scotland," *Charrette* 3, no. 1 (2016): 1–5. https://www.ingentaconnect.com/content/arched/char/2016/00000003/00000001/art00001

2 Jane Anderson & Colin Priest, "Developing an inclusive definition, typological analysis and online resource for Live Projects," in *Architecture Live Projects Pedagogy into Practice*, 2014, pp. 9–17.

3 Neil Burford & Carol Robertson, "Prototype Zero Energy Studio: a research-led, student-centred live build project," *Brookes eJournal of Learning and Teaching* 8, no. 1 and 2 (2016): 3–13.

4 Christiansson Jörn, Erik Grönvall, & Signe Louise Yndigegn, "Teaching participatory design using live projects: critical reflections and lessons learnt," *Proceedings of the 15th Participatory Design Conference* 1 (2018): 1–11.

5 C. Kraus, *Designbuild Education* (Taylor & Francis, 2017).
6 Richard W. Hayes, *The Yale Building Project: The First 40 Years* (Yale School of Architecture, 2007).
7 Jane Anderson & Colin Priest, *Live Projects Network*, accessed 1 December 2020, http://liveprojectsnetwork.org/about/
8 James B. Brown, "A critique of the live project," PhD thesis, Queen's University Belfast, 2012.
9 Chad Kraus, *Designbuild Education* (Taylor & Francis, 2017), p. 2.
10 James B. Brown, "From denial to acceptance: a turning point for design studio in architecture education," *Distance Design Education*, accessed 1 December 2020, https://distancedesigneducation.com/2020/05/11/from-denial-to-acceptance-a-turning-point-for-design-studio-in-architecture-education/
11 Sneha Gautam, 'COVID-19: air pollution remains low as people stay at home,' *Air Quality, Atmosphere & Health* 13 (2020): 853–857.
12 Eva Lloyd, "Early childhood education and care: poverty and access. Perspectives from England," in *The SAGE Handbook of Early Childhood Policy* (London: SAGE, 2017), pp. 268–286.
13 Lynda Schneekloth & Scott Shannon, "Easing boundaries through placemaking sustainable futures study abroad program," in *Service-Learning in Design and Planning: Educating at the Boundaries*, edited by Tom Angotti et al. (New Village Press, 2011), p. 185.
14 James B. Brown & Peter Russell, "Motivational misalignment: managing the competing drivers of trans-national design-build in rural South Africa," paper presented at *Building Beyond Borders: Reflecting on the Dynamisms of Intercultural Collaboration in Build Projects*, Hasselt University, 9–10 November 2020.
15 Carolyn Butterworth & Others, *A Handbook for Live Projects* (Sheffield: University of Sheffield, 2013).

2 Inspiring Public Imagination through a Micro Ecovillage for Students

Cameron Van Dyke

Introduction

I have been on a journey for the past five years that has caused me to question my own needs and expectations about the modern-built environment around me. I live in the United States and I daily experience the conflict between the individual goals of comfort, convenience, and consumption and the collective goals of sustainability, energy use reduction, and climate change mitigation. Acknowledging this conflict lies at the heart of any plan to improve the collective hopes for humanity. My biggest revelation over the past five years is that rather than focusing on technology as our hope for sustainability, it might be better to focus on how we could shift our individual values (and through that shift the values of culture) to desire a life of sustainability. That new life would replace the luxuries of personal comfort, convenience, and consumption with the luxuries of a more authentic and equitable relationship with the Earth and with others. Through a series of choices that challenged our typical suburban life, my wife and I experimented with downshifted living and discovered new luxuries we were not aware of. We wanted to share these discoveries with others and, since I am a university professor, it made sense to share them with students. The students came for a day, then for a week, and now for an entire school year to experience a different set of solutions in relation to our dwellings, our energy use, our community, and our interactions with the natural world. I would like to share with you a project that we are developing that encourages students to be reflective about their consumption, their impact, their cultural assumptions, and their future with the hopes of creating citizens willing to embrace needed change if sustainability is to thrive.

The Problem with Sustainability

There is very little these days that is sustainable about "sustainability." Every time a new electric car comes out or a new 5,000 square foot solar-powered home is built, we get excited that "sustainability" has triumphed. Unfortunately, this "sustainable" technology is still precariously propped up by unsustainable energy sources, resource extraction, and cultural expectations.[1] Sadly, I think most of us are more interested in sustainability as an ecological catharsis rather than in us actually acting in ways that are in balance with bio-physical limitations.[2]

What are we to do then? With 7.6 billion people on Earth, it would take a monumental shift (especially in industrialized societies) to act within sustainable limits.[3] There is a critical attribute needed to move things into balance and that is...restraint...both personal and collective.[4] However, I wonder if restraint is a natural condition for human beings (or for any life form for that matter). I propose that restraint is *not* natural and, therefore, it is not a reliable solution. A plant grows unrestrained until limiting factors stop it. Animal populations grow exponentially in the absence of limiting factors. I suggest that our modern society has overcome many of our limiting factors. Fossil fuels and industrialization have enabled the vast magnification of our normally limited human power. It is that magnification that enables humans to damage the earth in ways we do not anticipate.[5]

If restraint won't work, can we innovate our way into sustainability? Green technology is, of course, a positive advancement, but let's remember it was human innovation that made restraint necessary in the first place.[6] Green energy only serves to support our already consumptive mindset. Without a cultural shift that accompanies green technology, we will simply continue to grow until we encounter the inevitable limiting factors.

Therefore, if anything is going to alter the self-destructive path that humans are on, we need to replace our faith in both restraint and innovation with something more powerful, something like...aspiration! But how do we get people to aspire to something other than what they already know and want?

Public Imagination

This paper is titled "Inspiring Public Imagination through a Micro Ecovillage for Students," and I want to take a minute to explain what I mean by public imagination. We are familiar with the concept that to make change we must first visualize the change and then desire it. This is true on an individual level and at a societal level. Therefore, one of the big problems for the sustainability movement, or for the challenge of climate change, is that what most people visualize is something they do not desire.[7] What's visualized looks like inconvenience to us, or austerity to us, or God forbid, a challenge to the American lifestyle.

So, we need to change our behavior, but the question is...how do we create real change? I am reminded of the R. Buckminster Fuller quote: "You never change things by fighting the existing reality. To change something, build a new model that makes the existing model obsolete." The key to this quote is "positive replacement," and as a designer, I have adapted a particular approach in my work for disseminating the "new models" that Fuller speaks of. I practice "Speculative Design," which is a form of design that focuses on imaging to how things *could be* rather than responding to how they are.[8]

Typically, we think of design as a tool for problem solving, but design can also be used for problem finding. Typically, we think of design as affirmative of our cultural values (giving people what they want), but design can also be critical of cultural values. Typically, we think of design as being the handmaiden to an industrialized society, but design can serve to unravel the narratives of production and consumption.[9] The emerging subfield of "Speculative Design" was brilliantly codified in the 2013 book by Anthony Dunne and Fiona Raby, *Speculative Everything: Design, Fiction, and Social Dreaming*. They explain how this type of design often uses "future" or "fictional" constraints to experiment with possible new worlds to discover and promote preferable options or to imagine and warn about undesirable ones.[10] This approach could be described as using the language of design to do the work of art or storytelling. Specifically, the art of imagining the future and bringing those potential futures to life through prototypes in order to critique and test them. In regard to this imagining and prototyping, there is a particular technique that I use called "diegetic prototyping" to reach the public with new models. The term "diegetic prototyping" was coined by David Kirby in a paper titled "Future is Now – Diegetic Prototypes and the Role of Popular Films in Generating Real-world Technological Development."[11] (I highly recommend this excellent paper to anyone seeking to inspire social change.)

Kirby points out that films "construct cinematic representations of technological possibilities as a means by which to overcome obstacles and stimulate a desire in audiences to see potential technologies become realities."[12] He introduces the term "diegetic prototype" "to account for the ways in which cinematic depictions of future technologies

Figure 2.1 Orbit. Future Cycles project. The Future People 2015
Image by Cameron Van Dyke.

demonstrate to large public audiences a technology's need, viability and benevolence."[13] Stated in plain language, Kirby's paper looks at the way that film can be used to create acceptance in the public for products or ideas that would otherwise be foreign or rejected. By placing these new items or concepts inside a narrative, the filmmaker contextualizes the proposition with a history, taxonomy, and social value.

A great example of this is the 1950s film *Destination Moon*. We accept it as normal now that a person can go to the moon, but in 1950 the general public had no idea what that would look like and if it would even be ethical. The film *Destination Moon* was created by filmmakers and scientists to give an approximate depiction of what a trip to the moon would be like and to gain public support.[14] Kirby identifies three steps necessary for an audience to accept a proposition: first that the proposition is needed, second that it is physically viable, and third that it can be normalized inside of the culture.[15] I would add a fourth necessary step in that the proposition must also be desirable.

Kirby's paper is focused on how social change is achieved through the use of film, but I wondered if I could use the diegetic prototype technique directly in the real world as an agent of social change. As a person who designs and fabricates objects in real space and time, I wondered if I could possibly use this technique to both experiment with new prototypes for living and, at the same time, use those prototypes

Inspiring Public Imagination 29

to encourage others to expand their own sense of possibility. In other words…inspire public imagination.

I have been able to apply and test this technique in depth in my ongoing Future Cycles project in which I present self-built, low-energy vehicles, such as the Orbit (Figure 2.1), directly into public space.

In the speculative design community, this is defined as the discursive scenario,[16] where the object and the applied narrative come together to create the diegesis. The Future Cycles project has been a proving ground for a type of social practice that is a positive form of activism. It is inspirational and non-confrontational. It gains attention partially through spectacle but also in large part because of its authenticity. That is, unlike the film version of diegetic prototyping, I am creating real-world scenarios in which I actually design, build, and *use* alternative solutions to live my life. It turns out that doing this has tremendous power because in a world full of beautiful images of virtual objects, spin from news feeds with little credibility, and the general posturing of everything on social media, it is very impactful to witness a guy simply driving down the road in a sustainable vehicle that he built himself. In a world of subjective realities, that authenticity is refreshing. For the general public that direct experience hopefully creates an impact that moves the needle just a little more toward accepting and desiring needed change. Hopefully, the experience inspires just a little more public imagination.

Context of the Micro Ecovillage Project

I am an assistant professor of product and furniture design at Appalachian State University. The university is in the small town of Boone, North Carolina in the United States. We are high in the beautiful Appalachian Mountains with plenty of wild land nearby. My wife and I moved here after being suburban and urban dwellers for all our lives.

For the 2017–2018 school year, we decided to experiment with primitive off-grid living and moved to a cabin at Turtle Island Preserve on 1,000 acres of land. We lived mostly outside, collecting fuel for heat and cooking, walking a mile to feed the goats, and homeschooling our 11-year-old nephew (Figure 2.2). This was an intentionally challenging experience because (other than rustic camping for the weekend) we had never lived in way that was this primitive. We had to walk a quarter mile to get to the cabin from our vehicle and everything had to be hand carried – our water, our food, our tools, our building materials, and our furniture. We had to build our kitchen from scratch, and it was outside with no electricity and no plumbing. We had to care for

Figure 2.2 Life at Turtle Island Preserve
Photo: Cameron Van Dyke.

farm animals – which we had never done before – and additionally salvage some of the food for their two daily feedings. Our cabin was uninsulated and heated only by the large amount of wood we needed to collect from the forest around the cabin. There was no cell phone reception so our evenings were spent reading or playing games around the fire. I like to describe this nine-month experience as both wonderful and terrible. Wonderful because of the excitement of a brand-new relationship with our built environment, the animals, and the integral use of our bodies to meet our needs. Terrible because of the challenging relationship with our built environment, the animals, and the integral use of our bodies to meet our needs. The most interesting part of the experiment for me was realizing that although we gave up the modern conveniences of electricity, running water, and central heat (which was definitely a loss), we gained the luxuries of a direct experience of the weather, caring for animals, close proximity to each other, and meaningful physical labor. Our values profoundly changed through this experience and not only did we discover more joy and appreciation of life, but we also learned to live joyfully with a lot less material,

Inspiring Public Imagination 31

Figure 2.3 Students build wood storage racks
Photo: Cameron Van Dyke.

physical comfort, and energy consumption. We began to wonder if there was a way to share these discoveries with others – particularly the product design students that I work with – in order to allow them to make their own discoveries and, hopefully, shift their own values in the direction of true sustainability.

Developing the Micro Ecovillage Project

In January 2018, we purchased a steep vacant seven-acre wooded property close to the university in order to create a place that would allow us to continue to experiment with new sustainable relationships to housing and community, share our experiences with others, and promote new sustainable patterns of living to the public. From the beginning, we both wanted and needed students to be involved with helping us build it. We hired students to work and learn with us on all aspects of the project, working primarily on the weekends and over the summer.

32 Cameron Van Dyke

Figure 2.4 Sustainable Technology students fabricate a solar photovoltaic system
Photo: Cameron Van Dyke.

The process began by clearing trees from the building sites and creating a route for the driveway. We then hired a sawyer who sawed many of the trees into lumber. We built our first dwelling in the summer of 2018 with one student who was hired full time. Once we were back in session for the school year, students helped create outdoor living areas, built a rainwater catchment system, cut and split firewood, and created wood storage racks (Figure 2.3).

With the help of the Appalachian State Sustainable Technology Department, students designed and fabricated a solar photovoltaic system in order to provide electricity to the site (Figure 2.4). In our second summer, students were hired to create a terraced garden and assemble our second dwelling. Since then, students and I have built a small wood storage building and completed a third dwelling. Our infrastructure currently consists of three dwellings and all the off-grid systems that support them (Figure 2.5). At this time, we can accommodate three students living along with us on the project. We are currently working on a fourth dwelling and a fifth dwelling/common house with the goal of accommodating a total of eight people living on site.

Figure 2.5 Freshly completed student dwelling
Photo: Cameron Van Dyke.

Structure of the Project

As of now, the project is structured to be a free-standing private endeavor that is not funded by the university and there is no class credit given. The complexities of such an arrangement seemed daunting to me at the beginning as well as the fact that the project has *evolved* into what it currently is rather than was specifically planned. I also felt it was important to remain flexible to what is learned as we go along. Once we reach a stable size and presence, it may make sense to formalize a relationship with the university. For the time being, I am enjoying the freedom to explore the questions that develop from the experiment and share the organic evolution of the project with the students. In terms of financing, the project has been almost entirely self-funded by me and my wife. The investment has been fairly low because the dwellings are small and the students and I have done most of the work. The students do pay a small monthly contribution that is calibrated to be enough to sustain the project. There is no lease, and the students are free to move out whenever they like. We understand that there are many other pressures of being a university student, so we felt it was very important that the students have as much autonomy and flexibility as possible in this community. There is also no work exchange expected of the students other than to manage their own water and firewood supply and to pack out any waste they create. There are opportunities for the students to participate in the ongoing work of the project, however, and if they choose to get involved, they are paid a fair wage and I teach them the skills needed to do the various jobs. I design and plan the projects, but I remain open to the ideas of the students and often implement their suggestions.

In terms of physical logistics, we are entirely off the grid, so the students use wood stoves to heat their dwellings, use sawdust-filled composting toilets, and hand carry rainwater to their dwellings. There are no showers available on site, so students either create their own makeshift ways of cleaning up or they go to campus and use the student recreation center. We have just a little bit of electricity available from the solar photovoltaic system that is mostly used to power lights and a small refrigerator in each dwelling. We try to meet every week or two for a meal to touch base with each other, see how everyone is doing, and go over any logistical items for the community.

Inspiration and Precedence

I have had the great privilege to live in, visit, and learn from many intentional and educational communities over the years, and I owe a great debt to these experiences. In particular, I have been inspired by the Rural Studio of Auburn University. Their mantra remains "Educating Citizen Architects,"[17] which is the same focus I have adopted in educating "Citizen Designers" in the Applied Design program at Appalachian State University. Additionally, the physical aspects of this Micro Ecovillage Project have been inspired by the "Supershed and Pods" concept that the Rural Studio employs for some of its student housing. These student-designed and built structures test a variety of building concepts and, by living in these closely situated dwellings, the students come to understand the consequences of their predecessors' design choices.[18]

I have also been inspired by the work of Andrew Heben in his book *Tent City Urbanism: From Self-Organized Camps to Tiny House Villages*. This book chronicles the emergence of communities that use tiny dwellings to provide a low-cost/high-community-based residential experience for people who are traditionally housing challenged. The dwellings are often very basic but, like our project, the advantages of having a low cost, supportive community are empowering.

In particular, Opportunity Village in Eugene, Oregon, strikes a great balance of personal autonomy, responsibility to the group, and community support.[19] There are, of course, many other cohousing communities, ecovillages, and intentional communities that have informed or inspired what we are hoping to do in this project. You will find a list of those communities in the notes at the end of this paper.

Micro Ecovillage Goals

Using the lessons learned from the Future Cycles along with the many intentional communities that have inspired us, we are combining those concepts into this Micro Ecovillage project with the goal to establish a diegetic prototype and use it to create public imagination. That prototype is a small sustainable learning community that provides an alternative dwelling experience for the students that live on the project. It demonstrates to people who visit Kirby's three necessary steps for acceptance: we *need* to do this, it is *viable* to do this, and it is *normal* to do this. Additionally, it is our hope that we can demonstrate that it is also *desirable* to do this.

Our goals for the project are as follows:

1. To **discover** through firsthand daily contact new options for sustainable living
2. To **improve** those discoveries through iteration and prototyping
3. To **normalize** these new behaviors to be acceptable by the participants and the public
4. To **share** our experience with the public so that they might both imagine and desire the changes that we are demonstrating.

Through the Micro Ecovillage Project, our goal is to introduce people to a lifestyle option that, rather than being based on consumption, is based on participation with the natural world and others. Our hope is to help people discover new kinds of luxuries and new kinds of joys that are available because of this shift in values. Ultimately, we hope to inspire public imagination through a lived and shared experience.

Micro Ecovillage Purpose

This project challenges and replaces norms for typical student housing and suggests a very different set of physical solutions to the utility and community that student housing typically provides. It also challenges the typical balance of financial and personal investment – shifting from a typically high financial investment and low personal investment to the opposite: a low financial investment and a high personal investment. To be successful in the project, the students must make the jump from being a "consumer of housing" to being a "participant in housing." This is often a difficult transition as students initially consume the low cost, beautiful surroundings, and community meals without much thought to how the changing winter weather will affect their daily routines and their relationship with their dwellings. For those who never had anything but a thermostat on the wall and pressurized water that comes out of tap, it *is* a mental shift to have to plan and cultivate one's daily provisions. This is precisely one of the growth opportunities we are hoping for in the students' experience of living on the project. We hope to help them be more reflective and present, build perseverance, and more than anything become the kind of people that are willing to challenge their own expectations in order to discover improved ways of living. Our hope is to help people discover new kinds of luxuries and new kinds of joys that are available *because* of a shift to a more sustainable life. We are hopefully doing that for everyone that learns about, visits, or lives on the project.

Teaching and Learning Opportunities

Since 2018, over 175 students have toured the project, ten students have lived there for various lengths of time (up to nine months), and 35 different students have worked on the project – some for just one day, others for most of the summer. In all of these situations, I use the project as an extension of my teaching which integrates design skills and theory, sustainability, and citizenship. For those students that simply tour the site, I believe the learning impact has mostly to do with witnessing a way of living that is outside of the norm and that functions as a home for those who live there (a diegetic prototype that encourages public imagination). We also teach the student visitors about the systems that support the project (solar collection, rainwater harvesting, composting toilets, wood fuel, etc.) to provide a knowledge base that may open their minds to the necessary public shift to renewables and conservation. I also incorporate the ecovillage project into my model-making class where I use the site as the basis of an architectural modeling project in which the students design and fabricate a 1/24th scale model dwelling for a specific location on the site. Through this assignment, the students understand how to position a building relative to sun/weather/view/approach, apply appropriate structural and material language, and balance the required functions with good form. The fact that we are working with an actual site makes the assignment much more dynamic and grounds the learning in a tangible and memorable experience.

For the 35 students that have worked on building the various elements of the project, the learning comes from the instruction given to them to do the specific tasks at hand. Some tasks are physical in nature (splitting and stacking firewood), and others require some advanced thinking (carpentry or electrical wiring). Most of the students come from a suburban background and have little prior experience in any of the tasks that we need to do. I try to match new students with new tasks so that every work day that they participate in gives them new skills. One student worked for the summer building one of the dwellings from start to finish and, once the experience was over, he had developed enough skills to be hired on as a carpenter to a building renovation crew.

In terms of those students that live full time on the project, their growth comes from the long-term immersion in the lifestyle and systems of ecovillage living. They experience the prototype from the inside and adapt to or resist the elements of that life. They learn the mental skills necessary to navigate the sacrifices and benefits of this choice and also learn the physical skills of off-grid living, such as managing water and electric resources, collecting wood, finessing a wood stove for cooking and heating, and dealing with the discomforts of life with no plumbing or thermostat-controlled heating.

Student Impact

I believe that the impact on the students that live on the project is positive and lasting, and the best way to measure that is to hear from the students themselves. Here are some direct quotes from interviews with those students.

Josh (on his move out day): *"The fact that I was able to be so happy with such few things was an eye-opening experience. Cleaning the cabin today I am very sad to leave. I really do feel like this is an ideal way to live."*[20] (Figure 2.6.)

Jake: *"This is the first place I ever lived that I feel entirely comfortable. I can visually see my resources in front of me and it is so interesting to be much more directly connected to those resources."*[21] (Figure 2.7)

Dylan: *"It has made me reconsider my goals in life and I realize I don't need a large living space. As I picture my professional life, I am including things in that picture that I had not previously thought of."*[22]

Sydni: *"As far as moving forward it has put a lot of perspective into place of the lifestyle that I want. A lot of times it is easy to think I should*

Figure 2.6 Josh inside student dwelling #2
Photo: Cameron Van Dyke.

Figure 2.7 Outdoor area Jake and I built for student dwelling #2
Photo: Cameron Van Dyke.

have x, y, and z to be successful, but the way I view success now, because of this experience, has changed. I want to be present for my life. I want to live with the environment. I want to build things for myself and explore new avenues when something interests me. I want to get creative with making something for myself and have fun with it. I want to play with my life and I get to do that here and I don't ever want to stop doing that."[23]

Trevor: "I have learned that you really don't need a whole lot to live a great life. I was nervous moving into here, that I would miss the amenities. But, what do you need? What is a living situation? This is just a little off grid home in the woods. But I feel very comfortable in this tiny home. We have a few tasks like collecting firewood that each of us have to do regularly but it has become a part of the routine to where I think…this is good, this is normal, this is my home. It is simple, but I feel like that is the way it should be. You don't need so much."[24]

Brendan: "One of the experiences that really stands out to me is that very often when I am taking an outdoor shower a black-eyed junco bird will come and sit right next to me and bathe in the water that is splashing around. That's just one of those examples of how living like this has connected me to nature."[25]

It is encouraging to hear these responses and I believe they demonstrate a tangible shift that the students are experiencing because of their choice to experiment with this way of living. Another great part about having the students participate in the project is that they naturally share their experience with their own friends and family and bring guests to the project, thus increasing the impact without our direct involvement.

Conclusion

The Micro Ecovillage Project described in this chapter is not just a place where a professor and some students live in the woods but is hopefully a place that can be a prototype for a more authentic and equitable relationship with both the Earth and each other. It is a "living" laboratory that is both a test of new sustainable patterns of living and a demonstration to the public to inspire positive social change. Our project is a form of activism that is focused on a positive replacement of the status quo, the ultimate goal being to inspire public imagination for an environmentally and socially sustainable future.

My question to all of us, then, is this: As educators of young citizens, creators of the built environment, and proponents of sustainability, are we going to put our money where our mouth is? Let's lead by example and inspire people to imagine and desire a different kind of future that aligns with the bio-physical constraints of the Earth. Let's not just think sustainably, let's act sustainably and inspire others to join us.

Communities that have Informed or Inspired

Bruderhof Communities. Walden, New York, USA. https://www.bruderhof.com

Burlington Co-Housing. Burlington, Vermont, USA. http://www.bcoho.org

Camp Take Notice. Ann Arbor, Michigan, USA. http://www.missiona2.org & https://vimeo.com/47145016

Earthaven Ecovillage. Black Mountain, North Carolina, USA. https://www.earthaven.org

Frank Lloyd Wright School of Architecture. Scottsdale, Arizona, USA. https://theschoolofarchitecture.edu

Ganas Community. Staten Island, New York, USA. https://www.ganas.org

Homestead at Denison University. Granville, Ohio, USA. https://denison.edu/campus/homestead

Newberry Place Cohousing. Grand Rapids, MI, USA. https://newberryplace.wixsite.com/newberryplace

Rudolf Steiner Fellowship Community. Chestnut Ridge, New York, USA. https://www.fellowshipcommunity.org

Rural Studio of Auburn University. Newbern, Alabama, USA. http://ruralstudio.org

Square One Villages. Eugene, Oregon, USA. https://www.squareonevillages.org

Turtle Island Preserve. Boone, North Carolina USA. https://www.turtleislandpreserve.org

Well House Grand Rapids. Grand Rapids, Michigan, USA. https://www.wellhousegr.org

Bibliography

Berry, Wendell. *What Are People For?* New York: North Point Press, 1990.

Desilver, Drew. "How Americans are – and aren't – making eco friendly lifestyle changes." Pew Research Center, 2015. Accessed May 19, 2021. https://www.pewresearch.org/fact-tank/2015/11/17/how-americans-are-and-arent-making-eco-friendly-lifestyle-changes/.

Deyoung, Raymond and Princen, Thomas. *The Localization Reader: Adapting to the Coming Downshift.* Cambridge, MA: MIT Press, 2012.

Dunne, Anthony and Raby, Fiona. *Speculative Everything: Design, Fiction, and Social Dreaming.* Cambridge, MA: MIT Press, 2013.

Heben, Andrew. *Tent City Urbanism: From Self-Organized Camps to Tiny House Villages.* Heben, 2014.

Heffron, Alex. "Sustainability is not sustainable." Medium.com. Accessed May 17, 2021. https://medium.com/@AlexHeffron88/sustainability-isnt-sustainable-1b1547c3355.

Hopkins, Rob. "Energy decent pathways: Evaluating potential responses to peak oil." MSc. Dissertation, University of Plymouth, Plymouth, 2006. Accessed May 19, 2021. https://transitionculture.org/wp-content/uploads/msc-dissertation-publishable-copy.pdf.

Hursley, Timothy and Oppenheimer, Andrea. *Rural Studio: Samuel Mockbee and an Architecture of Decency.* New York: Princeton Architectural Press, 2002.

Khan, Tanzimuddin and Lynch, Tony. "Understanding what sustainability is not – and what it is." *The Ecological Citizen*, Vol 3 Suppl B (2020): 55–57. Accessed May 17, 2021 https://www.ecologicalcitizen.net/pdfs/v03sb-06.pdf.

Kirby, David. "The future is now: Diegetic prototypes and the role of popular films in generating real-world technological development." *Social Studies of Science.* New York: Sage February 2010, pp. 41–70. Accessed May 17, 2021. https://journals.sagepub.com/doi/pdf/10.1177/0306312709338325.

Martin, Roger and Kemper, Alison. "Saving the planet: A tale of two strategies." *Harvard Business Review*, April 2012. Accessed May 18, 2021. https://hbr.org/2012/04/saving-the-planet-a-tale-of-two-strategies.

Rural Studio of Auburn University. Accessed May 19, 2021. http://ruralstudio.org.

Tharp, Bruce and Stephanie. *Discursive Design.* Cambridge, MA: MIT Press, 2018.

Notes

1 Tanzimuddin Khan and Tony Lynch, "Understanding what sustainability is not – and what it is," *The Ecological Citizen* Vol 3 Suppl B (2020): 55–57, accessed May 17, 2021, https://www.ecologicalcitizen.net/pdfs/v03sb-06.pdf.

2 Alex Heffron, "Sustainability is not sustainable," Medium.com, accessed May 17, 2021, https://medium.com/@AlexHeffron88/sustainability-isnt-sustainable-1b1547c3355.

3 Rob Hopkins, "Energy decent pathways: Evaluating potential responses to peak oil," MSc. Dissertation, University of Plymouth, Plymouth, 2006: 19–22, accessed May 19, 2021, https://transitionculture.org/wp-content/uploads/msc-dissertation-publishable-copy.pdf.

4 Roger Martin and Alison Kemper, "Saving the planet: A tale of two strategies," *Harvard Business Review*, April 2012, accessed May 18, 2021, https://hbr.org/2012/04/saving-the-planet-a-tale-of-two-strategies.

5 Wendell Berry, *What are people for?* New York: North Point Press, 1990: 7–8.

6 Tanzimuddin Khan and Tony Lynch, "Understanding what sustainability is not – and what it is," *The Ecological Citizen* Vol 3 Suppl B (2020): 7–8, accessed May 17, 2021, https://www.ecologicalcitizen.net/pdfs/v03sb-06.pdf.
7 Drew Desilver, "How Americans are – and aren't – making eco friendly lifestyle changes," Pew Research Center, 2015, accessed May 19, 2021, https://www.pewresearch.org/fact-tank/2015/11/17/how-americans-are-and-arent-making-eco-friendly-lifestyle-changes/.
8 Anthony Dunne and Fiona Raby, *Speculative Everything: Design, Fiction, and Social Dreaming*, Cambridge, MA: MIT Press (2013): 1–9.
9 Anthony Dunne and Fiona Raby, *Speculative Everything: Design, Fiction, and Social Dreaming*, Cambridge, MA: MIT Press (2013): 1–9.
10 Anthony Dunne and Fiona Raby, *Speculative Everything: Design, Fiction, and Social Dreaming*, Cambridge, MA: MIT Press (2013): 1–9.
11 David Kirby, "The future is now: Diegetic prototypes and the role of popular films in generating real-world technological development," *Social Studies of Science*, New York: Sage, February 2010, accessed May 17, 2021, https://journals.sagepub.com/doi/pdf/10.1177/0306312709338325.
12 David Kirby, "The future is now: Diegetic prototypes and the role of popular films in generating real-world technological development," *Social Studies of Science*, New York: Sage, February 2010, accessed May 17, 2021, https://journals.sagepub.com/doi/pdf/10.1177/0306312709338325, 41.
13 Ibid.
14 David Kirby, "The future is now: Diegetic prototypes and the role of popular films in generating real-world technological development," *Social Studies of Science*, New York: Sage, February 2010, accessed May 17, 2021, https://journals.sagepub.com/doi/pdf/10.1177/0306312709338325, 57–59.
15 David Kirby, "The future is now: Diegetic prototypes and the role of popular films in generating real-world technological development," *Social Studies of Science*, New York: Sage, February 2010, accessed May 17, 2021, https://journals.sagepub.com/doi/pdf/10.1177/0306312709338325, 42–44.
16 Bruce and Stephanie Tharp, *Discursive Design*, Cambridge, MA: MIT Press, 2018: 185–208.
17 Rural Studio of Auburn University, accessed May 19, 2021, http://ruralstudio.org.
18 Timothy Hursley and Andrea Oppenheimer, *Rural Studio: Samuel Mockbee and an Architecture of Decency*, New York: Princeton Architectural Press, 2002: 71–72.
19 Andrew Heben, *Tent City Urbanism: From Self-Organized Camps to Tiny House Villages*, Heben, 2014: 156–164.
20 Josh, interview with author, October 28, 2020.
21 Jake, interview with author, September 2, 2020.
22 Dylan, interview with author, November 21, 2020.
23 Sydni, interview with author, July 9, 2021.
24 Trevor, interview with author, October 23, 2021.
25 Brendan, interview with author, October 24, 2021.

3 Moving from Learning to Doing

An Educational Experience of Temporary Tactical Action

Silvia Tedesco, Elena Montacchini, Tommaso Ferraris and Carlotta Gerbino

Introduction

The paper describes an educational experience of tactical urbanism in the city of Turin (Italy) developed in the framework of a student team called AUT (Autocostruzione Urbanismo Tattico), at Politecnico di Torino. AUT is a "place" to build architecture in a real environment through hands-on activities carried out by the students in cooperation with academic tutors and by involving a network of external stakeholders.

The reference context is linked to changes in the way contemporary architecture and the city are conceived: from static and almost eternal, to changing and transforming.[1] In order to tackle the social and economic problems that afflict our cities, such as the accentuated degradation of the suburbs or the progressive weakening of social inclusion policies, it is increasingly necessary to rethink the mechanisms and tools traditionally used for urban regeneration, not only by practitioners but also by citizens.[2] Today, in fact, ephemeral realities, often supported by groups of citizens and local associations, are joining forces with permanent ones, collaborating to create a dynamic urban fabric. Temporary spaces are growing in the city and are in continuous transformation over time, providing an answer to the unsatisfied needs of those who live there every day.[3]

This paper, through the description of an educational experience of temporary tactical action, intends to reflect not only on the value of this "practice" for the physical and social regeneration of abandoned or underused urban areas but also on the role of the Schools of Architecture in promoting educational experiences aimed at a new generation of architects, capable of dealing with these issues and taking the field with tangible actions, moving from learning to doing.

DOI: 10.4324/9781003267683-4

Around an Experience: Two Keywords, Two Aims

The experience described below focuses on two main topics – temporary tactical actions and the learning by doing approach – both connected with the AUT Team's background and its path to self-constructing a microarchitecture for the reactivation of an abandoned green area.

In fact, the aim of this research is twofold:

- to develop new solutions for the transformation of fragile urban spaces, for their physical and social reactivation
- to experiment with a new practical learning model to empower architecture students, by exploring a new form of pedagogical relation between university and society, and involving a network of stakeholders into academic training through the realization of self-constructed architectures for the transformation of fragile urban spaces.

Temporary Tactical Action

Urbanism is defined as tactical when it can operate through "a healthy balance of planning and doing".[4] This means combining traditional large-scale planning and long-term policies with "acupuncture"[5] actions that promote the possibility of inhabitants to participate and redesign the city through micro-transformation, co-management, and care of spaces and services in their neighborhoods, and therefore to contribute to the construction of shared urban development scenarios.[6]

For these reasons, temporary tactical actions – short-term, low-cost, and scalable interventions – are a growing trend all over the world: urban spaces are increasingly used as an experimental ground where art, architecture, and activism are intertwined to create future scenarios in a physical and social regeneration perspective. Temporary tactical actions are well defined as *"short-term actions for long-term change"*[7] and allow the promotion of the Agenda 2030 goals related to social sustainability and urban regeneration, including a wide variety of very eclectic practices, different in size, purpose, time, and actors involved: from the ephemeral architectures of young multidisciplinary architectural studios to temporary shops, to spontaneous urban community gardens or pop-up plazas promoted by local administrations.[8]

Consequently, to guide these new urban transformation processes, it is clear how today even the profession of the architect demands an adaptation of roles and crafts.

Over the past decade, collectives of architects have emerged whose work combines architecture, urbanism, public art, and self-construction. Their projects, which fit into international networks to support tactical actions, become a testing ground for new forms of interaction between inhabitants and urban spaces.[9]

Learning by Doing Approach

As defined by Bruce and Bloch,[10] learning by doing is "the process whereby people make sense of their experiences, especially those experiences in which they actively engage in making things [...]".

In the academic field, there are exemplary cases of ambitious and revolutionary teaching methods that have based their effectiveness on a totally practical approach to architecture, involving students in hands-on activities: from those of Peter Fattinger (Vienna University of Technology)[11] to those of Rural Studio (Auburn University School of Architecture, Planning and Landscape Architecture).[12]

The MSc degree course in Sustainable Architecture at Politecnico di Torino is adopting such new learning methods by proposing concrete challenges to the students through guided approaches, with the aim to experiment with new teaching and learning modalities and, moreover, provide answers to the real needs of society.

We consider practical activities, often conducted on real scale models, a way to combine theory and fieldwork. Practical activities are both training and research experiences: they represent an opportunity for deeper and more effective knowledge and learning; they allow the development of students' soft skills; they make it possible to verify the feasibility of solutions and technologies, supporting processes of innovation; they promote the generation of synergies between different disciplinary areas; they identify new areas of experimentation and research.

In the specific context of this work, we will describe the learning by doing approach that was adopted as an educational tool to experiment with architectural choices and construction processes related to a temporary architecture built in a public space.

AUT

A Student Project Experience

AUT is an acronym for Autocostruzione Urbanismo Tattico, or Self-construction Tactical Urbanism. To better illustrate the work of AUT, it is necessary to describe the background that the authors of this paper based this project on.

When thinking about the final year project at the end of architectural studies, a sense of inadequacy toward architecture practice pervaded some students, making them feel unprepared to enter the real world of work after graduation. For this reason, Politecnico di Torino is introducing alternative teaching proposals to the traditional ones of theoretical and design courses. The aim is to complement student training through a different, more hands-on type of learning, aimed at developing the design skills that are typical of the architectural profession.

The input to conceive AUT was born after attending an optional university course, a professionalizing workshop called A.R.C.A.[13] (Art, Research, Community, Living), held by professor Regis D. together with local cultural associations and the support of groups of professionals. The field experience, which consisted in concretely responding to the needs of a community through the construction of a temporary structure to catalyze social and cultural events, was fundamental to start reasoning on what could be the contribution of two architecture students to such cause.

The answer came from the opportunity that Politecnico di Torino gives to many types of student activism: a funding program[14] that supports teaching and entrepreneurial activities proposed by students every year through the presentation of structured programs supported by professors and partners, with detailed cost estimates and periodic reports. In fact, the funding is granted through an internal call for proposals of the university, for which the student groups enter a list of activities related to their field of studies that present some character of innovation and a business plan to realize them. Therefore, thanks to these circumstances it was possible to recruit interested students and participate in the Politecnico call, obtaining a large part of the requested funds.

Today AUT consists of a design-and-build workshop[15] conducted by 11 university students and recently graduated architects. It is performed thanks to the Politecnico funding program and coordinated by the founders Carlotta Gerbino and Tommaso Ferraris. More specifically, it is organized as a self-led group of students, with professors – who act as coordinating supervisors – from different Politecnico departments, including Architecture, Design, and Engineering, to make the most of different skills (Figure 3.1).

The Team Activities

AUT is a "protected reality" to build architecture in a real environment through hands-on activities carried out by the students in

Figure 3.1 AUT's students sitting on Tablò, the structure realized during the first workshop
Photo by the authors.

cooperation with academic tutors, by involving a network of external stakeholders interested in collaborating with university initiatives. Its main goal is to give students the freedom to experiment, to develop new professional skills, and to gain concrete experiences as a contribution to their academic preparation while taking full responsibility for simple architectural processes by acting directly on the territory and cooperating with numerous entities such as fragile communities, administrations, associations, professionals, and so on.

Primarily, the task of the student team is to offer different kinds of cultural activities open to students and included in the annual schedule, varying from the more strictly theoretical and research ones – such as meetings, conferences, interviews, and competitions of ideas – to practical ones such as self-construction workshops. Indeed, AUT periodically organizes talks with distinguished professional practices, which are fundamental moments of exchange concerning research on temporariness, tactical urbanism, civic activism, and self-construction: "*Do It Yourself Architecture. L'architettura effimera a servizio della rigenerazione urbana*" *(ephemeral architecture for urban regeneration)*.[16] The conferences that took place on April 12 and December 6, 2019 at Castello del Valentino in Turin included presentations of the experiences of international firms such as Collectif ETC,[17] Camposaz,[18] Archistart,[19] and also of other students' associations such as Acropoli[20] or Recyclo.[21] These sharing opportunities were precious to understand the importance of the increasingly widespread practices of self-construction with the involvement of citizens aimed at improving life and places of collectivity.

"The process of making is more important than the project for its own sake".[22] precisely for this reason, the practical activities proposed by AUT consist of self-construction workshops led by students and professional tutors to gain direct all-around experiences of real light interventions and increase their skills by getting involved directly, creating a strong network between university, communities, and the professional world.

An exemplary case of involvement and participation is a recent project carried out by the team, called Col-Legno. Col-Legno[23] is a workshop organized by AUT that took place in February 2020 in Collegno (Turin), in a learning garden named "Orto che Cura". The garden is held by a social cooperative, Il Margine, that deals with reintegrating people with social difficulties or physical and mental disabilities. The process, guided by the team, lasted four months and it involved the garden's community in the design and part of the construction. It completely transformed an uncultivated outdoor space into an organized learning garden, while improving its overall quality and accessibility.[24]

The professionalizing workshops proposed by AUT are usually recognized by Politecnico di Torino by offering university training credits (or "CFU") to students, proportional to working hours, thus encouraging participation in these types of training activities that go beyond the academic university programs.

A Project: Tablo'

Among AUT's goals, one of the most important is to realize small-scale projects in fragile urban spaces while creating a network of local stakeholders by working together with professionals, citizens, and administrations, inside and outside the University. The opportunity to do so was given by the imminent reopening of a historical municipality-owned social hub in the center of Turin's main park. The research team involved not only students and teachers but also architecture studios, public institutions, associations, and many local artists, activists, and supporters.

How it Started: The Context and the Municipality Call

The 2019 City of Turin call for summer events[25] for the reactivation of underused urban green areas was the opportunity to get involved in the transformation of a public space. AUT took part in a winning proposal submitted by a network of associations to organize summer events in a place of great social value, in the middle of the most famous park of the city, which was going to reopen at that time; as students of architecture, the purpose was to build the temporary structure that could host the entire schedule of public events and connect the park to the building.

The participation of AUT in the entry for the City of Turin call favored the selection of the proposal by the committee, as it represented an innovation compared to the ordinary event organization method, by having a group of architecture students realizing their own design of a temporary structure, hosting a number of different events open to the public, and adding architectural quality and social value to a construction that, alternatively, could have been merely a prefabricated, budget object serving its mere function. Moreover, the team had the support of Politecnico di Torino, which definitely helped in gaining trust and credibility from the stakeholders involved in the project.

On the Po riverside, *Parco del Valentino* is the most popular park of Turin and takes its name from the XVI century castle that lies in its heart, which currently hosts the School of Architecture. At the beginning of the 20th century, the park hosted two different World Expositions, with many temporary pavilions being constructed in the area: evidence of the latter can be found in cafés, clubs, and restaurants scattered around the park.[26] However, in the past decade, many such places have been closed over disputes between the municipality and the tenants, causing abandonment and social decay in various areas of the park. Many of the structures that once hosted restaurants, cafés, and clubs were trashed and illegally occupied by abusive dwellers, and the park started to be known as "dangerous". One of the most iconic buildings is the *Imbarchino del Valentino*, a historic social hub, built in the late-19th century, an embarcadero transformed into a café that soon became the focal point of the park's social and cultural life.

The latter is a complex that develops on three different levels and connects a large lawn with the Po River below. It is formed by a main building that hosts the café and all the main facilities, a warehouse that became a place for indoor events, a pier, and many green areas, some well-used, others less. In particular, directly in front of the

Imbarchino del Valentino there is a lawn which is one of the city's most important gathering points due to its central position. It offers a panoramic view of the river and green hills behind it, forming a sort of a natural bleacher with a scenic backdrop.

The *Imbarchino del Valentino* is owned by the municipality and is given in temporary management to associations and companies by public tender. It closed in 2016 and in the same year it was destroyed by river floods and vandals. However, in 2019 a network of associations managed to find an agreement with the municipality to restore the facility and reopen it starting from the summer of that year. These associations have been the promoters of the City of Turin call for summer events in which AUT participated and that led to the realization of the project described below.

Design Phase

The design phase is a crucial and highly formative phase for students in self-construction projects because it forces them to translate an idea into a real object, to conceive the best succession of construction phases while considering the economic aspect too.

In the beginning, the team carried out a series of on-site inspections together with the managers of the project area to identify the needs of the "client". It was fundamental for AUT that this activity was not only finalized at the construction of an architectural object, but that it was a moment of training and professional growth for the students involved, by taking responsibilities and by having to face the choices made in the design phase hands-on. The students have made a shared path as a team, with a horizontal and anti-hierarchical organization that, through brainstorming sessions and study of design references, has led to the design of various possible solutions until the final project was reached. Through meetings and discussions, and after weighing out several possibilities, the team arrived at a synthesis able to combine a concept with a strong identity with the various functions and features considered suitable for a project in this specific context.

The student team led the project in every phase of its evolution, which lasted around four months; however, AUT strongly believes that in order to learn how to create a high-quality architecture, students must be advised by professionals with real experience in the field. For this reason, Orizzontale,[27] a collective of architects from Rome that focuses on design-build and temporary architecture in the public space (Young Talents of Italian Architecture at the Venice Biennale in 2018) was assigned a tutorship role. Orizzontale followed the design phase through various reviews and weekly video calls where

Moving from Learning to Doing 51

they advised students both on the concept and its relationship with the context, and on the more constructive and executive aspects of the construction of a wooden structure with the characteristics we had planned. With their expertise, they led the student team throughout the most critical aspects of the design phase, showing alternatives or better solutions to what they planned and allowing them to identify their latent design intentions while at the same time respecting AUT's ideas and decisions. Orizzontale's fundamental contribution finally culminated in its presence during the week of the realization of the structure, when it coordinated the construction site and guided the practical work, sharing knowledge and techniques important for professional growth with the students.

During the executive design phase, AUT had to consider the Building Regulations of the City, looking for a uniform definition of urban planning and building parameters that would regulate a structure like the one it was going to build, but there was no trace of it. The building regulations for construction in the public space are very strict in Italy, even more so in a historic park like *il Valentino*, which has many constraints that require various levels of approvals by different public authorities.[28] Specifically, within the Park, the new buildings are subject to landscape constraints and subject to the approval of several bodies, including the City of Turin, the Soprintendenza Archeologia Belle Arti e Paesaggio (authority for archeology, fine arts, and landscape),[29] and the Ente Parco del Po Torinese (park authority for the Turin Po River area),[30] with approval times of several months that would lead to a lengthening of the project incompatible with the timing imposed by the circumstances.

Unable to deal with the overwhelming bureaucracy, the team decided to refer to the "free building activity",[31] which in case of public events allows the construction of *"structures of limited size and not permanently fixed to the ground"*,[32] *"with no fixed roof or connection to the ground, for a maximum of 90 days, after which the structure must be dismantled"*.[33]

However, retrospectively we can say that these difficulties along the way allowed the AUT team to understand which aspects of the project should have been excluded from the design to avoid bureaucratic issues, and define other solutions instead, both from the structural and the functional point of view.

The bureaucracy definitely hindered the process, since the project did not fit entirely in any of the categories foreseen by the law, but it was positioned more in a blurred line between them. Instead of seeing this as a limit, the team embraced the difficulties and the problems related to the policies and the regulations: the design phase took into account all of the legal and practical constraints. The structure is composed of wooden dry-assembled frames with modular movable furniture and a totally removable roofing system consisting of a tailored white scaffolding shading cloth. The structure and its furnishings are simply free-standing on the ground, and – strictly with screw fixtures – they are designed to be easily disassembled in a short time when necessary. For the reasons listed above, AUT decided to create a hybrid space that is built within the perimeter of the venue, but at the same time, it is purposely facing outwards, communicating with the large public lawn in front of it with the dual function as a space for events but also a place for leisure.

Construction Phase

As shown by many Italian and European experiences of temporary interventions for the re-activation of public spaces, one of the most effective tools to recruit motivated builders is the community construction site organized through open calls for students and locals interested in the uses of such places or their role in their communities. In fact, to carry out the project AUT organized a self-construction workshop open to students, architects, designers, or anyone interested in taking part in the process. A public call was launched in June 2019 through events on social media and advertising flyers posted on university and cultural hub notice boards. After having scheduled the construction timing and calculated the necessary number of people for the activities to be carried out properly, a group of 15 builders was selected among students of architecture, design, engineering, recent graduates, and professionals in the field, depending on their skills, workshop experiences, and motivation letters.

As scheduled, the construction site lasted one week, under the guidance of Collettivo Orizzontale together with the members of AUT and the supervision of the coordinating professor. In the same days, important renovation work was taking place inside the Imbarchino del Valentino, for which a building site was set up with the presence of several workers. This required an accurate plan to divide the spaces and avoid any interference between the two working groups and any hazard for the people in the area. Moreover, since AUT was working on the street level, close to the passage of people in the park, we experienced a lot of curiosity and questions about our work and the imminent reopening of the building. Somehow AUT's presence and its structure became a sort of an advertisement landmark for the space and eventually it was the first sign for the people that the Imbarchino del Valentino was open again to the public after many years (Figure 3.2).

Moving from Learning to Doing 53

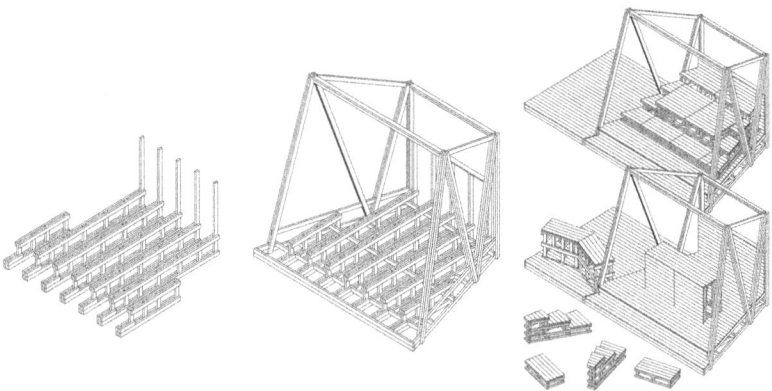

Figure 3.2 The construction phases of the structure
Image by the authors.

The workshop was carried out in two construction phases: the off-site production stage and the on-site production stage.

The first phase took place in the technology laboratory of the University, the LaSTIn,[34] a space dedicated to all experimentation activities carried out by the teams or by single students for specific Thesis projects, which is equipped with all the tools for the processing of building materials, especially the raw natural or sustainable ones.

On the first day, a safety course was held to teach everyone the necessary safety measures and the correct use of tools, and after that the building area was set up in the external space of the laboratory, where the students stocked and prepared the material. During the first two days, the work consisted in performing preliminary processes to the rough four meters long fir wood, such as: cutting with the miter saw, sanding, spreading the impregnating agent, and doing a pre-assembly of the structural frames of the stage and furniture.

The second phase started in the next few days. The working site with all the tools moved to the project area, at Imbarchino del Valentino, where the students started to install the frames that were transported on site. The construction developed as follows: first, the supporting frames were adapted to the natural irregularities of the soil and aligned among them; second the M-shaped elevation structure of the sides was assembled and fixed to the stage; and lastly both the stage and the furniture frames were completed with planed boards, while a complementary lower platform was built adjacent to the main one. The structure was entirely dry-assembled with self-threading Torx screws, and

Figure 3.3 The construction site's activities
Photo by the authors.

it was completed with a totally removable shading roof system, which was designed on-site by sewing a white scaffolding shading cloth with borders and perimeter eyelets, useful for hooking it onto the elevation frames (Figure 3.3).

The final result is a flexible stage that was called *Tablò*, "painting" in the local dialect, precisely because it develops like an optical cone, a scenic backdrop that frames the landscape behind it. This concept has been suggested by the location itself, in an attempt to channel the viewer's eye toward the structure and, behind it, the scenic view of the Po river and its hills. The main stage, with its trapezoidal shape, is completed by an accessory side platform and a set of modular furniture that can form different shapes for different functions, depending on the occasion. This idea of structure versatility was a focal point of the project because of the need to accommodate many different uses of the space across the different moments of the day and night.

Use and Aftermath

During the summer, this small intervention helped to bring the area from an initial state of abandonment and disuse to an active and dynamic situation, with DJ sets, drama performances, concerts, lectures, yoga sessions, and more unforeseen citizens' activities. In addition to this, as hoped, *Tablò* became one of the most popular places of *Imbarchino del Valentino,* even when there were no planned events, and people simply liked to use it as a place for leisure, for having a drink or a meal outdoors, using its modular furniture as benches and tables and enjoying its privileged position in the Parco del Valentino. Thanks to the new conditions of use that temporary interventions can suggest, this forgotten place was reclaimed by the citizens, regaining its importance in the park and the city, in an impulse to the urban regeneration that we hope can continue in the future.

After the 90-day period of use required by the regulations was over, and once the summer events for which Tablò had been purposely created had finished, the structure was disassembled by the AUT team. However, with a perspective of future reassembly, all the pieces and the various components have been carefully numbered, cataloged, and stored in a warehouse inside the Imbarchino del Valentino.

Given the success of the structure, which over time has become a recognizable landmark in the area, the managers of the space saw to starting a dialogue with the authorities to obtain the necessary permits to proceed with reassembly of the structure the following year, with the intention to keep it installed for an indefinite period of time, that is until the natural life of a wooden structure exposed to the elements is over. In this way, it became operational and open to the public not only in the summer but year-round.

For these reasons, the following spring, in the year 2020, AUT returned to the project site to proceed with reconstruction. The operation was completed in a very short time thanks to the very accurate instructions elaborated during the first disassembly, but it still presented some criticalities that taught the students some issues to take into account when planning such operations. For example, the holes of the screws had widened excessively in some cases, not allowing a solid assembly: in these cases, we inserted new screws at different points, which led to some slight misalignments compared to their original position. Moreover, it required additional efforts to allow correct positioning of the planks, since wood is a living material, and some of them had curved or had swelled due to the humidity of the river.

The reassembly of Tablò was made more complicated by an event that happened in the fall of 2019, when the structure was disassembled and stored in the warehouse: in fact, the Imbarchino del Valentino was hit by a major flood of the Po River that, among other damages, also covered with water the wood of the structure for about three days. After this event, the boards were cleaned and dried in the sun, but the fabric cover made during the workshop was lost during the flood. In any case, even after being re-assembled the structure is back in operation and continues to be a popular spot in the area.

AUT's collaboration with this particular area went beyond. In the summer of 2021, the team organized a new workshop that led to the creation of a second structure: a long, shaded tunnel used as an open-air studying space, called *Corridò* (a contraction of the word "corridor", "corridoio" in Italian), which was built of wood with a PVC roof. The prolonged collaboration with the managers of the space confirmed the appreciation of the work developed by the students for the park users. This new creation contributed to the students' acquisition of new professional skills and competencies, which had important implications in their design abilities (Figures 3.4 and 3.5).

Figure 3.4 Before...
Photo by the authors.

Moving from Learning to Doing 57

Figure 3.5 ... and after
Photo by the authors.

Results and Conclusions

The innovative aspect of this experience, based on the independence of the student action, is the development of responsibility and awareness in the design of a real-life case, which have led to new professional skills as well as an "architectural self-confidence" that arises from the direct construction. Moreover, the tactical intervention shows how it is possible to transform an urban space with low-cost but high-impact actions and helps to understand the new tools available to the profession of the architect.

In particular, the workshop was very useful to share knowledge and discuss methods of action, especially essential for new workgroups preparing to face similar experiences in the future. It has taught the students to be aware of the problems that arise when trying to do something that goes beyond traditional teaching.

In general, this experience results in a win-win for students, academics, public authorities, and society. Not only did it let the students take full responsibility for the process and learn how to realize and manage a small-scale project, how to harmonize architecture experimentation with technical aspects, and how to respond to real needs and respect urban plans, transforming a design exercise into tactical civic action, but also led to the development of a sense of participation and strong relationship with the human capital of the context in which they have worked. By funding student initiatives, Architecture Schools can play a proactive role in civic involvement, improving the quality of urban life as well as opening new opportunities to upgrade competencies and connect universities, professionals, and communities. Moreover, on one hand, these activities make it possible to experiment with new ways of teaching that are not feasible in a university classroom, and on the other, they offer advantages for public authorities and society related to the physical and social regeneration of underused areas.

This type of experience is definitely a powerful training opportunity that needs to be further discussed, as it would help to overtake the caesura that exists nowadays between architectural education and professional practice. However, a strong criticality emerges from this experience, related to the lack of legislation on educational building activities on site. In fact, the rules to be respected and the roles of each actor of the educational innovative practice are still not clearly defined, thus both bureaucratic processes and professional relationships with external entities represent fundamental cruxes to be solved to simplify these types of teaching activities. By debating on some of the institution's examples of similar works (such as M.A.A.C.C., a bivouac for cycle tourism self-built by the student team Recyclo, we also came to realize that sometimes the difficulties are so big that they often lead to radical modification of projects, and even to lose their purpose with their reduction to school exercises and projects for their own sake.

Sometimes the rigidity of the regulations to which interventions that are light, simple, temporary, and easy to disassemble are subjected seems disproportionate to their purpose, and often for safety reasons it is not permitted to entrust students with the use of several mechanical machines, which can only be operated by specialists. Above all, it would be necessary to define a balanced relationship between risk, responsibility, result, and output of architectural objects that are not meant to last long, but that generate strong effects and stimulate public initiatives.

Therefore, we are often able to notice that the feasibility of formative practical activities has to deal with bureaucratic and regulatory aspects that are not so easy to overcome. However, it must be acknowledged that they have great potential not only as learning methods and strengthening tools for future architects but also as possible scenarios for the progressive transformation of weak urban spaces through tactical inputs and complementary strategies.

In conclusion, two interesting issues should be considered: the training one, well explained by the Archistart motto "start to be an architect", and the performative one, which clearly expresses that all the people who participate in the initiatives would love the projects to turn into reality. Perhaps we all have the ambition that what we achieve does not remain only physically, but that it also has a real social implication. The question we leave pending deals with these two aspects: how can we provide training and produce real objects, which can really work?

This experience of a temporary tactical action carried out by AUT shows just one of several plausible strategies to answer this complex question. Experimentation through research and reworking of effective participative project methods is the road we are taking toward the implementation of the learning by doing criterion, trying to relate an innovative educational system with its direct application to reality, that would be able to conciliate university, local authorities, communities, and stakeholders. Surely the know-how and the characteristics of each place or situation always condition the development of these types of processes. This is why analysis and research have to keep on experimenting with new opportunities to respond to the new challenges of innovation in teaching.

Bibliography

Acropoli website. Accessed January 28, 2021, https://www.acropolitrento.com/.

Archistart website. Accessed January 28, 2021, https://www.archistart.net/.

AUT. "DIY Architecture" Talk organized at Castello del Valentino, Politecnico di Torino, Italy, April 12, 2019.

AUT website. Accessed January 7, 2021, https://autarchitettura.wordpress.com/.

"Bando per le manifestazioni Estive 2019", Comune di Torino. Accessed January 28, 2021, http://www.comune.torino.it/bandi/pdf/files/avviso_pubblico_manifestazioni_estive_2019.pdf

Bazzu, Paola, and Talu, Valentina. *Tactical Urbanism – Italy*. Sassari: TaMaLaCà, 2016.

Berni, Francesco. "Il riuso temporaneo come pratica innovativa di rigenerazione urbana". *Urbanistica Informazioni* 263 (2015): 9–10.

Berni, Francesco. "Il riuso temporaneo come pratica innovativa di rigenerazione urbana". *Urbanistica Informazioni* 263 (2015): 10–17.

Bianchi, Cesare. *Il Valentino: Storia di un Parco*. Torino: Il Piccolo Editore, 1984.

Bohn, Maxence. "DIY Architecture: Collectif ETC" Talk organized at Castello del Valentino, Politecnico di Torino, Italy, April 12, 2019.

Bruce, Bertram C., and Bloch, Noemi. "Learning by Doing". *Encyclopedia of the Sciences of Learning*. Springer, Boston, MA, 2012. accessed January 20, 2021, https://doi.org/10.1007/978-1-4419-1428-6_544.

Camposaz website. Accessed January 28, 2021, https://www.camposaz.com/.
Chiappero, Floran. *Du Collectif Etc aux "collectifs d'architectes": une pratique matricielle du projet pour une implication citoyenne*, Aix-Marseille Université, 2017.
Collectif ETC website. Accessed January 28, 2021, http://www.collectifetc.com/.
"Col-Legno", AUT. Accessed January 26, 2021, https://autarchitettura.wordpress.com/2020/09/15/.
"Col-Legno workshop: all'orto che cura, un team studentesco del Politecnico di Torino al servizio della progettazione sociale", Orto che Cura. Accessed January 25, 2021, https://www.ilmargine.it/orto-che-cura-attivita/
DM 2/3/2018, n° 43–50 "Glossary containing a non-exhaustive list of the main works that can be carried out under the regime of free building activity", Building Regulations of the City of Turin, n° 37–42.
D.P.R. 31/2017, A.16–17 "Regulation identifying interventions excluded from landscape authorization or subject to simplified authorization procedures".
D.P.R. 380/2001, art. 6, comma e-bis-...-quinquies "Unified text of laws and regulations on construction".
Ente Parco del Po Torinese website. Accessed October 8, 2021, http://www.parcopopiemontese.it/.
Fattinger Orso Architektur, "Design build studio". Accessed January 20, 2021, http://www.fattinger-orso.com/.
Ferraris, Tommaso and Gerbino, Carlotta. *Spazio Temporaneo: La quarta dimensione come strumento progettuale*. Torino: Politecnico di Torino Master's Thesis, 2019.
Lerner Jaime, *Urban Acupuncture*. Island Press, London, 2014.
Lydon, Mike, and Garcia, Anthony. *Tactical Urbanism: Short-term Action for Long Term Change*. Island Press, Washington, DC, 2015.
Orizzontale website. Accessed January 8, 2021, http://www.orizzontale.org/.
Polytechnic of Turin website. Accessed January 28, 2021, http://www.politoward.org/sw2018-1/2018/5/23/progetto-maacc-team-recyclo.
Progetti Studenteschi PoliTO. Accessed January 22, 2021, https://didattica.polito.it/pls/portal30/sviluppo.ateam.elenco_progetti?p_lang=IT#114
Rural Studio website. Accessed January 20, 2021, http://ruralstudio.org/about/.
Soprintendenza Archeologia Belle Arti e Paesaggio website. Accessed October 8, 2021, http://www.sabap-to.beniculturali.it/.
"Tactical Urbanist's Guide". Accessed January 20, 2021, http://tacticalurbanismguide.com/guides/.
ZOOART A.R.C.A. Accessed January 26, 2021, https://www.art-ur.it/progetto/zooart-arca-2018/.

Notes

1 Ferraris T. and Gerbino C., "La città temporanea: spazi e pratiche a tempo determinato" in *Spazio Temporaneo. La quarta dimensione come strumento progettuale* (Torino: Politecnico di Torino Master's Thesis, 2019), 69–147.

2 Francesco Berni, "Il riuso temporaneo come pratica innovativa di rigenerazione urbana", *Urbanistica Informazioni* 263 (2015): 10–17.
3 Ferraris and Gerbino, *Spazio Temporaneo. La quarta dimensione come strumento progettuale*, 119–121.
4 Lydon M. and Garcia A., *Tactical Urbanism: Short-term Action for Long Term Change* (Washington: Island Press, 2015).
5 Lerner J., *Urban Acupuncture* (London: Island Press, 2014).
6 Bazzu P. and Talu V., *Tactical Urbanism – Italy* (Sassari: TaMaLaCà, 2016).
7 Lydon and Garcia, *Tactical Urbanism: Short-term Action for Long Term Change*.
8 "Tactical Urbanist's Guide", accessed January 20, 2021, http://tacticalurbanismguide.com/guides/.
9 Chiappero F., *Du Collectif Etc aux "collectifs d'architectes": une pratique matricielle du projet pour une implication citoyenne* (Aix-Marseille Université, 2017).
10 Bruce B.C. and Bloch N., "Learning by Doing", *Encyclopedia of the Sciences of Learning* (Boston, MA: Springer, 2012), accessed January 20, 2021, https://doi.org/10.1007/978-1-4419-1428-6_544.
11 Fattinger Orso Architektur, "Design built studio", accessed January 20, 2021, http://www.fattinger-orso.com/.
12 Rural Studio, accessed January 20, 2021, http://ruralstudio.org/about/.
13 ZOOART A.R.C.A, accessed January 26, 2021, https://www.art-ur.it/progetto/zooart-arca-2018/.
14 Progetti Studenteschi PoliTO, accessed January 22, 2021, https://didattica.polito.it/pls/portal30/sviluppo.ateam.elenco_progetti?p_lang=IT#114.
15 AUT website, accessed January 7, 2021, https://autarchitettura.wordpress.com/.
16 AUT, "DIY Architecture" Talk organized at Castello del Valentino, Politecnico di Torino, Italy, April 12, 2019.
17 Collectif ETC website, accessed January 28, 2021, http://www.collectifetc.com/
18 Camposaz website, accessed January 28, 2021, https://www.camposaz.com/
19 Archistart website, accessed January 28, 2021, https://www.archistart.net/
20 Acropoli website, accessed January 28, 2021, https://www.acropolitrento.com/
21 Politecnico di Torino website, accessed January 28, 2021, http://www.politoward.org/sw2018-1/2018/5/23/progetto-maacc-team-recyclo
22 Maxence Bohn, "DIY Architecture: Collectif ETC" Talk organized at Castello del Valentino, Politecnico di Torino, Italy, April 12, 2019.
23 "Col-Legno", AUT, accessed January 26, 2021, https://autarchitettura.wordpress.com/2020/09/15/.
24 "Col-Legno workshop: all'orto che cura, un team studentesco del politecnico di torino al servizio della progettazione sociale", Orto che Cura, accessed January 25, 2021, https://www.ilmargine.it/orto-che-cura-attivita/.
25 "Bando per le manifestazioni Estive 2019", Comune di Torino, accessed January 28, 2021, http://www.comune.torino.it/bandi/pdf/files/avviso_pubblico_manifestazioni_estive_2019.pdf
26 Bianchi C., "Il Valentino: Storia di un Parco", Turin, Il Piccolo Editore, 1984.
27 Orizzontale website, accessed January 8, 2021, http://www.orizzontale.org/

28 D.P.R. 31/2017, A.16–17 "Regulation identifying interventions excluded from landscape authorization or subject to simplified authorization procedures".
29 Soprintendenza Archeologia Belle Arti e Paesaggio website, accessed October 8, 2021, http://www.sabap-to.beniculturali.it/
30 Ente Parco del Po Torinese website, accessed October 8, 2021, http://www.parcopopiemontese.it/
31 D.P.R. 380/2001, art. 6, comma e-bis-...-quinquies "Unified text of laws and regulations on construction".
32 DM 2/3/2018, n°43–50 "Glossary containing a non-exhaustive list of the main works that can be carried out under the regime of free building activity".
33 Building Regulations of the City of Turin, n°37–42.
34 Laboratorio Sistemi Tecnologici Innovativi (Innovative Technological System Laboratory) of the Polytechnic of Turin.

4 Training Future Architects through Professional Responsibility

Working with Real Cases in the Master's Degree in Architecture at Vallès School of Architecture

Marta Serra-Permanyer and Roger-Joan Sauquet Llonch

Introduction: The Opportunity of the Hinterland

Traditionally, schools of architecture have studied the hyper-urban territory. In the case of Catalan schools, Barcelona has been the main area of work. Tourism territories, especially on the coast, are also profusely investigated. Students have developed hundreds of proposals ranging from urban studies to specific building projects. But there is an imbalance between a highly populated city like Barcelona, widely considered by architects and urban planners (local authorities also have agencies that carry out urban studies), and a rural or semi-rural space, which needs more investment in urban reflection and intervention due to a lack of resources from the authorities. On a demographic level, there is a trend towards depopulation, motivated by lack of opportunities, that contrasts with the municipalities of the metropolitan belts that gain inhabitants. However, rural territories are essential in matters such as renewable energy, food sovereignty, global biodiversity, and environmental equality.

This inland territory – rural, semi-rural, or ex-industrial – offers an opportunity to be worked on by architecture schools. On the one hand, students and researchers find this hinterland full of possibilities, in which any architectural idea is practically a novelty. Likewise, they find a population, some political representatives, and some technicians from the public authorities willing to listen to any proposal that improves the territory and reverses its tendency to decline. For a

DOI: 10.4324/9781003267683-5

teaching methodology such as the Vallès School of Architecture (ETSAV) Master's Degree in Architecture seeking co-responsibility for the work of their students trying to improve their impact, these territories are extremely relevant.

Vallès School of Architecture enjoys a proven track record in relation to its commitment to socio-ecological responsibility applied to the territory. The school has participated in and received awards at different Solar Decathlon competitions[1] together with some other Design Studios that have engaged in service-learning at the bachelor's degree level. Nonetheless, this is not a sole or unique tradition since several international-related experiences[2] within the academic field can be identified. A specific literature review on architecture, participation, and pedagogy[3] depicts a number of academic initiatives among which the most outstanding are located within non-European countries, for instance the Rural Studio in the United States but also Ciudad Abierta in Valparaíso and Talca University, both in Chile. All of them display a catalogue of examples that the Vallès School has been able to learn from.

Main Pedagogical Objective

Within the Vallès School of Architecture, the Master's Degree in Architecture is an "enabling" master's; a tool of the Spanish University system to professionally qualify architects through one extra year after the compulsory five years of the bachelor's degree. In Spain, universities have the competence to train professionals to assume responsibilities that, in the case of architects, are very broad, from structural calculation to urban planning. Passing this enabling master's is mandatory for those graduates willing to practise professionally as architects and urban planners.

There is a regulation that defines the conditions of access to official university teaching and sets out a list of competences established by the Spanish architecture schools, included in Royal Decree 1892/2008. Some of the competences are the following: "The ability to understand the profession of architect and their social function in society; the development of projects that take into account social factors; knowledge of how to apply criteria of sustainability and social commitment in architectural solutions; the ability to exercise architectural criticism; adequate knowledge of the history and theories of architecture, as well as related arts, technologies and human sciences; the ability to understand the relationships between people and buildings and between them and their environment; adequate knowledge of methods used to study social needs and quality of life; knowledge of the architectural, urbanistic and landscape traditions of Western culture, as well as its technical, climatic, economic, social and ideological foundations; aesthetics and the theory and history of the fine arts and applied arts; the relationship between the cultural patterns and the social responsibilities of the architect; urban sociology, theory, economics and history",[4] among others.

These competences attributed to the university system were interpreted by the teaching team of the ETSAV master's degree as an opportunity to explore the concept of responsibility. The objective is to work with reality, so that students can take responsibility for their own proposals, interacting with the usual interlocutors of any architectural project such as the developer, municipal technicians, and residents.

In this sense, the idea of service-learning fits perfectly with this objective and working in rural and semi-rural areas makes it easy to do so. On the one hand, agreements with the public authorities of these territories allow real urban problems to be tackled, in which it is easy to capture the opinion of the people through participatory workshops. And on the other hand, the work of students returns to the territory at the end of every master's course, bringing new ideas to their problems, widening people's knowledge of them, and highlighting investment opportunities for governmental or private actors. Such an impact is expressed in different ways: through public exhibition sessions of the student projects, through an online publication published on the websites of the master's and the authorities, and through the commitment of the public authorities to carry out and materially develop one or more actions planned by the students.

Methodology and Structure

Within the framework of an experiential cycle of the Service-Learning Agreement, the structure of the master's is composed of a three-fold perspective: it is a real case, it works towards implementing a 1:1 scale, and finally, it involves community interaction towards the notion of transformative participation.[5] Each strand defines its own methodology to be developed in parallel and at different intensities depending on the nature of the location, its conditions, and the approach of the students.

Open Process: Actions towards Uncertainty and Change

A thesis by Richard Sennett on public space argues that closed structures of the organization have paralysed urbanism, whilst open ones might free it. The sociologist defines living organisms as harmonious ecosystems or habitats where their components are related through exchange, dependence on equilibrium, and integration. By contrast, he describes social systems as open structures defined by diversity, complexity, change, and exclusion, which are always able to adapt and mutate under very adverse conditions.

In his essay *The Public Realm*, Sennett explained that widespread urbanism intervenes in the city as if it were a closed system, as if it applies design with control and rigidity. He also adds that forcing equilibrium in a social order can sacrifice dissent for the sake of harmony.[6] Therefore, the master's gives advice to allow the appropriation or unforeseen use of the space by means of some project guidelines: looking out for the time dimension and phases, thinking small, integrating whatever already exists, reversibility, awareness of current socioeconomic conditions that might change, achieving a certain degree of fuzziness and, above all, the containment of the "ego" or mitigating the desire to create something new without a specific reason.

From this approach of the condition of openness, in *Planning Unplanned* the researchers Holub and Hohenbüchler presented a series of artistic strategies to offer another angle for looking at things, providing different perspectives for reframing the problem and broadening the context to new and open strands of research.[7] Some of them rely on the ability to visualize processes and conflicts, make the process the result itself, the chameleon-like spirit to adopt different roles and borrow external methodologies or even the spirit of finding cracks that legitimize the intervention. All these make the project an agent in itself for gathering, transforming, and issuing non-expected new meanings and expressions.

Borrowing these contributions from the field of art and from social studies, some projects in the master's degree have fostered interventions to embrace uncertainty and change. As an example, a couple of students have tried to reactivate the heritage of the ruins of an abandoned church. With the help of local residents, the students celebrate an act of symbolic foundation to demand civic appropriation and public investment. This specific intervention is the result of awareness of the role of unpredictable variables that guide the projects through an open process.

Social Return: Participation at Two Speeds

Social return is inextricably linked with community participation. Participation can be defined as a condition by which the individual being becomes part of a set or form of multiple associations; it is a category that varies in time and space. According to ethical and political trends and positions, the term may receive a wide range of denominations, but in any case, it is a cultural construction that takes us into the field of the social. According to the French philosopher Louis Lavelle, to exist is to participate freely of being, living is discovering one's vocation, and the person is the result of an act of participation, freedom of invention, and self-realization.[8] Moreover, the word participation comes from the Latin noun "pars" that means each one of the things that result from dividing a thing, that is, that a part together with other parts make up a whole, a larger unit to be integrated into, to feel included in. This larger unit is what we refer to by the denomination "social", as if it were a matter of scale. However, the French sociologist Bruno Latour[9] (2008) explains that two very different meanings coexist when it comes to addressing the meaning of "social":

First, the social sciences have described the "social" as an adjective, as a specific quality or property that can be attributed to something and that is used to establish explanations of causality and effect. That is, the social can explain "why", the social may be the reason for many questions that architects ask. In this case, the agents are always within this social context that encompasses them, and this determines a separate relationship between the investigated object and the investigative subject. Second, and in opposition to the first approach, Latour proposes another form of critical understanding where the "social" does not have any specific conditions, does not represent any context or domain of reality because things are not social in themselves, and does not belong to a "social" whole in the vein of Lavelle. According to Latourian critical sociology, social is a form of relationship, a form of ordering, it is nothing material, it is a link. It is a form of association that adds different heterogeneous elements. It is a relationship rather than an object. This fosters the conception of space in a relational way, a changing uncertain space, constituted as a network where the actors do not have to be "social", they can even be immaterial.

In consequence, for this Master's Degree in Architecture, referring to "social return" allows an understanding of the existence of relational space and the role of its own agency. The connections between context and content are not unidirectional and the students are expected to become aware of the position they play within the network of actors and immaterial "actants" they belong to. Overcoming the distance between the observer and the object of research and understanding the observer as a personal account – since recent theory demonstrates how the observer is present and affects the situation – has become one of the main goals of the methodology applied to the course.

Yet the pedagogical effort is aligned with the following challenges: "How can we conceptualize architecture differently? How can we make accounts of architectural objects and practices without falling into the trap of the abstract divides nature/culture, society/architecture? What is the alternative to critical architecture?"[10] To do research into this endeavour, the course offers exercises of listening, observing, registering, and interacting at two different speeds or rhythms:

On the one hand a slower pace: transversal participation, a collective process, where all the students are involved and learn to work as a large group. The methodology handled is based on Participatory Action Research (PAR),[11] originated in the 1940s and revised in the 1970s from the social psychology of Kurt Lewin and Fals-Borda.[12] The PAR involves three fundamental aspects that fit with the academic project in the architecture workshops: it focuses on identifying and working with a user group or community that experiences a specific concern; this community participates in research, that is, it is involved in decision-making based on determining priorities; and finally the research is aimed at generating improvement actions and problem-solving that develop a critical conscience on the part of all the actors involved.

The criticism we exercise in this process means contrasting, overcoming latent stigmas and inherited roles, facing paradoxes, questioning our own voice as architects, raising controversies, recognizing ambivalences and resistance that exist from the point of view of those who design and make decisions at the same time.

The process is very close to the "Die Baupiloten Methods" proposed in *Architecture is Participation*[13] with the whole group of students going together through the stages required in a participatory process (co-diagnosis, co-design, validation, and return) (Figure 4.1). Some of the purposes of this collective process are: to bring the results of the public workshops into the project definition when designing; to facilitate the students to develop the role of catalyst, since they activate projects and participatory processes; and at the same time, to act as "transducers", a term taken from the theory of social networks and presented by the contribution *Transducers: Collective Pedagogies and Spatial Politics*. Its authors explain how a transducer is "a device able to transform or convert a certain type of input energy into a different type of output energy, causing complex growth. Transducers are ecological in character, as they are directly involved in the context they change".[14] In other words, the students experience how they are affected by the change of perception of reality when approaching people.

In parallel, the second pace: the individual one, the one where each group of students designs their own process of participation

Training Future Architects through Professional Responsibility 69

Figure 4.1 Participatory design workshop between students and citizens, Cardona, 2018
Photo: Marta Serra-Permanyer.

and schedules their own strategies for involving the stakeholders. It is thanks to the collaboration with these actors that some students manage to self-build their projects at this stage. Within this individual pace, the students tend to make use of different ethnographic techniques and social qualitative research. They work by creating focus groups, holding interviews, developing participatory observation, and record keeping. The students also take advantage of contacting professionals that may give advice in the specific field of their case study. Research in historical archives and contact with local entities that may contribute to the memory of the place also intervene in this process. The search for referents in participatory design for similar projects is also essential to provide more security and methodological rigour.

As an example, a group of three students designed a skate park in an old square, having scheduled their own participatory process with different stages not only with the future users but also with professionals and technical advisors when defining all materials for the building process.

As an exercise in deep listening and through a series of oriented interviews on-site, another group of students tried to understand the

Figure 4.2 "Artisan cheese factory and kindergarten" project, by Aina Santanach and Meri Mensa, Sant Bartomeu del Grau, 2016–2017
Photo: Aina Santanach and Meri Mensa.

needs and desires of a couple of young farmers who had recently moved to the countryside to build a self-managed kindergarten and an artisan cheese factory, thus taking advantage of the academic project in a period of general economic crisis and scarcity of means (Figure 4.2). The project was developed through a series of face-to-face interviews and cognitive maps with the young couple. The students put all their efforts into expressing the fulfilment of the couple's life project and into adjusting to their budget and ability to generate income. They also visited some existing factories related to artisan cheese production. The case was very useful to illustrate that interaction in community design does not consist of "giving a voice" but in the act of activating

Training Future Architects through Professional Responsibility 71

deep listening. In particular, this project finished with a pilot study based on a new self-built construction to create the kindergarten. The couple's low budget and the use of local materials (straw) became the main strategies to implement the design by self-building after a long and individual process of creating trust between students and users. The teaching team accompanied the process from a proper distance so that students could face the necessary risks to integrate real learning.

In whichever rhythm is applied, participation is a way of intervening that is based on achieving transformation and change, not only in what is supposed to be our job but also in our way of seeing reality. Henryk Skolimowski, author of *The Participatory Mind*,[15] declared that to change the world we have to change the way we think about it and perceive it. That is why participation is research, it is learning to analyse the questions that we ask ourselves or that come to us through a project.

Physical Experimentation: From Decision-Making to Self-Building

One of the keys to the assumption of responsibility by the students is that their projects get to be built. Juhani Pallasmaa, in his book *The Thinking Hand*, determines that physical work is essential for a craft like architecture.[16] This phenomenon does not occur in every intake in a supervised way, but the master's offers opportunities for it to occur. We can highlight two different built interventions that have come about in two intakes of the master's degree. The first comes from the students' relationship with the owner of a farmhouse and is an example of the potential autonomy of the user and mutual aid. The second comes from an official commission from a city council to the master's students.

The first case is currently located in Sant Bartomeu del Grau, a so-called micro-village with a large number of scattered farmhouses. In the 2016–2017 intake, the master's degree was implemented in this municipality and many students found project opportunities in the farmhouses. In them, the students worked on topics such as the water cycle, the improvement of the living conditions of livestock or the treatment of waste.

The students Iñigo Ocamica and Iñigo Tudanca made their base at the Mas Vilanova farmhouse (Figure 4.3). In it they discovered an inefficient irrigation system and aging facilities, as well as an opportunity for co-habitation. Their project was based on an accurate analysis of the farm as an ecological system that includes a water cycle, biomass

Figure 4.3 "Mas Vilanova" built project, by Iñigo Ocamica and Iñigo Tudanca, Sant Bartomeu del Grau, 2016–2017
Photo: Iñigo Ocamica and Iñigo Tudanca.

cycle, and production cycle related to energy expenses – adding these topics to the fact that the farm is also an inhabiting system itself. The aim of the project was to conceive the farm as an autonomous and sustainable ecosystem, balancing the water sources, and the biomass generation capacity of the estate with the dimension of its vegetable garden. Analysis of the water cycle detected ancient infrastructures used for the storage of rainwater, which is very irregular throughout the year in this region. Some of them leveraged the runoff water from paths and roads. Other infrastructures made the most of rainfall by constructing ditches. The proposal aims to recover these elements, modernizing them, and adding new ones that make this water use more efficient. Some of the new elements that influenced the improvement of the water cycle were small reservoirs located under the renovated

Training Future Architects through Professional Responsibility 73

houses, a large new outdoor pond, and a whole network of newly built channels that allowed the orchards to be irrigated without leaks. The project also included small repairs in parts of the farmhouse important for self-sufficiency in basic necessities, such as chicken coops and small stables, as well as the access paths to the orchards.

The opportunity to build a small part of the project arose from the relationship that they maintained with the owners during the master's degree. Specifically, the owners facilitated the building of an irrigation pond and a chicken coop, the most urgent items to tackle. The owners provided the material, while the students, with the help of more colleagues, provided their own labour. Over several weekends they were able to finish the two constructions. The pond was built with concrete blocks, which were assembled and completed in a very short time. Concrete blocks offer a very affordable material which is available from any construction warehouse in the area. The chicken coop was also built with affordable materials such as wooden poles, steel cables, and galvanized mesh. The students recorded the entire process. Using time-lapse video, they captured the process of building the pond and produced a large number of photographs and shorter videos. This audiovisual material was used to defend their project at the end of the course, which they completed with honours.

The second built project shows the result of design and work direction practice through public funding (Figure 4.4). The 2018–2019 intake of the master's degree was rather unique because it was commissioned to adapt and improve the conditions of the entire Llobregat riverside in the municipality of Sallent, in the Barcelona region. The city council specifically commissioned the school of architecture to carry out this task and it was conveyed through the master's degree. This municipality had turned its back on the river throughout its history. On the one hand, the river was the dumping ground for the industrial facilities that had been located on the riverbank since the mid-19th century. On the other, it was at the back of the houses in the town that used river water from their backyards to irrigate their domestic gardens. The abandonment and demolition of some of these industries, plus the construction of a new bridge in the city, highlighted the deterioration of the river and the need to relate to it, now as a large green and civic space for the people of the town.

The river was therefore a space of opportunity to generate a linear park that took advantage of the landscape and climatic conditions, especially in summer. The students were organized in groups and in total 14 projects were planned along the river. Some projects were parks, others consolidated old vestiges of abandoned industries,

Figure 4.4 "Oasis" built project, by Álvaro Alcázar, Roser Garcia, Eduard Llargués and Sergio Sangalli, Sallent, 2018–2019
Photo: Álvaro Alcázar del Águila.

others improved accessibility to this low-lying land of the town. Finally, the city council chose five projects that were carried out. Most were built by municipal technicians with the help of the students. And one project, called "Oasis", the largest one, was led by a team made up of a master's professor, the main coordinator, who assumed civil responsibility, and the four authors of the project.

The "Oasis" river park project had two main aims: on the one hand, to bring the neighbours closer to the river through a permeable riverbank forest. On the other hand, to control the effects of flooding by determining floodable areas within the park that expand the flow capacity of the river in this section. The elements of the project were very basic: the modification of the topography, the planting of riverside vegetation, and the layout of the roads. The role of the students during the construction process was very similar to that of a professional architect on a construction site: direct the work and make decisions in the event of changes or unforeseen events. The role of the teachers and professors, who assumed responsibility for the work, was to arbitrate between the construction company and the students in case of difficulties, support them in case of doubts or any lack of technical knowledge, and maintain contact with the town hall.

The construction was full of anecdotes, but perhaps the most remarkable was the flooding of the park when it was almost finished. Despite being a flood with a return period of 100 years, the park performed brilliantly and demonstrated its successful design. With this teaching activity, the students acquired skills that surpassed the common competences of the master's degree: knowledge of the profession, managing a finite budget (in this case around 200,000 euros), agility in decision-making, teamwork, and the ability to adapt to changes. The proposal won the Young Talent Architecture Award[17] that evaluates Final Degree Projects. The jury precisely highlighted the value of these extra learnings that are obtained when trying to carry out an architectural project to its last consequences.

The third project shown is a proposal which was not built but which also had consequences beyond the master's degree. The edition of the master's degree for the 2019–2020 academic year was located in the town of Cardona,[18] an important Catalan municipality with a notable medieval old town. Salt was the main focus of interest in the municipality since the Neolithic age, as it had a saline diapir that allowed the extraction of table salt from the surface. Therefore, Cardona was always a strategic enclave in the territory, a fact that explains its imposing and important castle. Geological discoveries in the early 20th century showed that there was a large amount of salt rich in potash under the diapir. Potash was a more valuable product than salt and the saline valley was exploited with a mine that was in operation until the 1990s.

The abandonment of the mine added to an abandonment of industrial activity that is typical of globalization, causing the town to enter a decline that led to depopulation. Cardona now has 4,500 inhabitants, half the number it had in the 1980s. The most dramatic evidence of this depopulation is the situation offered by the medieval old town, an interesting and important urban area subject to strict heritage protection regulations. The obsolescence of its buildings, with very narrow and tall plots, and the extreme slope of the streets generate multiple accessibility and habitability problems. Apart from the loss of inhabitants, the medieval old town also loses economic and commercial activity. In addition, abandonment generates risk situations due to the collapse of facades or entire buildings.

The master's degree intervened in this panorama of decline to try to find architectural solutions that improve the situation of degradation. The projects located in the medieval old town provided a collection

Figure 4.5 Medieval old town of Cardona, 2018
Photo: Marta Serra-Permanyer.

of solutions both to improve urban accessibility, with interventions to the public space and to improve the habitability of homes, with interventions in the old buildings (Figure 4.5). The conclusion of this sum of interventions was that the plots had to be grouped to find gaps that allowed the urban area to be permeabilized both vertically and horizontally. Publicly displaying the results of the course to technicians and residents showed that there are solutions but they may conflict with the heritage regulations. It is, therefore, a worrying paradox that, in part, the harshness of protection regulations is the main reason for the destruction of heritage.

This important and desperate paradox has motivated the creation of a commission that has to work beyond the master's degree, sitting different authorities down at the same table in order to find a solution either by modifying the regulations or by finding management figures that facilitate the grouping of plots and inhabitants. In this commission received by the school of architecture, the participation of students who made proposals for the medieval old town is expected. Although they have already graduated, these students have the chance

Training Future Architects through Professional Responsibility 77

to make their project, or part of it, reality and will contribute all the knowledge accumulated during a year of research and proposals to the commission. Learning, therefore, can continue for these students through mediation work, adapting the proposals to new realities and investigating through the trial-and-error binomial, raising the influence of their academic work to the possibility of improving a whole urban area. The authorities consider this commission, which combines the possibility of modifying regulations with that of generating urban management figures, to be a pilot test that can be replicated in other municipalities that have similar problems.

A Critical Approach: Discussion on Current Challenges

Some students define the master's degree stating that it consists of a real commission with a real client and in real-time. However, and in past intakes, teaching staff and coordinators have been aware of the need for a critical approach and revision of the capacity to accomplish the purpose.

The first overview recalls the meaning of "responsibility" and the challenge of its assessment. As for C. Greig Crysler, "Architecture schools are locations where expertise is produced and exchanged, in this case through the pedagogical experiences of design/build".[19] And referring to H. Lefebvre, society produces space, but society is produced by the space itself.[20] If so, the commitment or responsibility of the schools of architecture in the social production of the built environment is dialogical as well. "Responsibility" is a key term within our course's vocabulary, tackling the need to be consistent, accountable for one's actions. Looking up its Latin etymological root,[21] it broadens its scope towards the commitment to give a feasible answer, to respond as a promise in return to any given idea. This means it will not be easy to ask accurate questions since the question has to be followed by a feasible answer. For the master's, this has become a must, and unrealizable expectations are strongly warned against. Nonetheless, very few projects reach the self-building stage, and these are very difficult to compare and evaluate with those that have not tried to reach this stage, stopping at a comfort zone and producing a standard project. Even so, some projects that do not opt for the self-building stage may well have developed and experienced the condition of responsibility based on raising awareness of and greater rigour in all factors that ensure the viability of the project in a future scenario. As seen, the meaning of responsibility may cover a wide range of senses and may be expressed in a number of different ways. And even more, the main challenge has been to identify from what position we judge the capacity of success or failure of these projects. In consequence, the design studio of the master's has identified ten topics that fulfil the main goal of achieving professional responsibility through the work in real cases. They are as follows: critical overview, identification of opportunity and pertinence; urban and regional planning consideration; adaptability and response to social ensemble; environmental awareness and care; cultural and material heritage approach; coherence between the proposal and activities, uses and programme; introduction to economic feasibility; link between technical and constructive design; harmony between elements and aesthetic intent; and finally, representation and communication effectiveness. Some other criteria regarding technology are also assessed.

The second on-going challenge consists of finding a method to monitor the impact of the built projects on-site. The integration and transformation of the works in the field require monitoring and a periodical incursion on-site that exceeds the time calendar and resources of the course and each intake. Once they are architects, the former students are the ones responsible for keeping track of the progressive evolution of the work, either in a public work or in a private intervention. But the need and interest to integrate this stage have become evident for the qualitative information it might generate. So far, the master's has activated an official yearbook to be delivered to the institutional agents involved, such as Barcelona County Council as well as the different municipalities participating in the Service-Learning Agreement. Public sessions to explain the results to citizens have also been developed and the three-fold agreement between the School of Architecture, County Council, and City Hall pursues the implementation of at least one project. Trust between these three parties is a determinant in guaranteeing long-lasting and sustainable results. The role of private stakeholders and the involvement of civic associations may be essential as well. The management of time according to political agendas and internal biorhythms and the way the School of Architecture displays results become another key issue.

And third, we should mention the resilience of the programme to current and unpredictable change. The arrival of Covid-19 has put up a series of unexpected barriers to be overcome. As a response to conditions imposed by contact and mobility constrictions, the programme has adapted to a virtual classroom format and in consequence the field work regarding community involvement has almost been dissolved. Direct contact and exploration with the place have hardly developed and the programme has been forced to re-address its experiential dimension towards a more speculative research project. The dependence on mobility to reach the hinterlands of the Barcelona region has not helped during 2020 and 2021. During this period, the course has not made a commitment to digital participatory tools. This decision was deliberate and duly considered with its pros and cons. It could have been a fresh opportunity to introduce new technologies for decision-making, but it would also have required prior research and pilot tests that would have been difficult to integrate with the academic schedule. In addition, it might have represented a barrier for some participating local communities and much more dedication on the part of the local technical mediators. In short, we are committed to not distort the practice of participation in non-assumable purposes. In consequence, we try to highlight the power of the ritual of personal contact, of the confrontation and encounter of bodies and languages. The course was able to restart face-to-face meetings in autumn 2021. Thus, participatory design has been carried out as a direct learning exercise again.

Concluding Remarks

Working with real cases in this master's degree in architecture has been the proposal to achieve the goal to train future architects through professional responsibility. The exploration of the methods applied and the discussion of results allow a simple conclusion to be made: the spirit of responsibility developed by the projects in this master's involves overcoming the fear of introducing changes or making mistakes when we start working in a different way to how we have learned. This statement is a demand for change, a change affecting architects but also the chain of actors who might be key players in co-design processes: politicians, government technicians, consultants, industrialists, builders, bricklayers, consumers, architecture critics, teachers, and students. All of them are questioned by a need for cross-cutting change.

At the same time, the desired and expected responsibility is constituted by a sort of fragility and opportunity, it is not innocent, it has its own agency. And this agency encourages the right to question and forges freedom of thinking and critical distance to those future architects we accompany. From the teaching perspective, it is an opportunity to re-educate our professional way of looking at things when it comes to managing control and fear of change and represents an opportunity to practise empathy and recognize in others the reflection of our own otherness.

Furthermore, as Paul Hirst[22] argues, if the University trains intellectuals capable of engaging in a political and cultural regeneration, it cannot afford to stray very far from people's concerns. In this sense, the question of responsibility implies a project of a heuristic nature that can support and accompany this purpose. But the penetration of the more complex bases of "responsibility" in architecture studies will depend on the degree of demand of the teaching staff when it comes to stimulating the gaze of the architects that we train as well as pursuing a deep and critical reflection for a rigorous and effective implementation.

And finally, as stated by Robert Goodman[23] in his publication *After the Planners*, the responsibility of the architect no longer rests with being the "outside" expert who tries to solve needs. On the contrary, the architect is another participant in the community itself. As proposed by this master's degree, the architect may become part of the process of the collective creation of physical devices that stimulate the development of new forms of life.

Bibliography

Balcazar, Fabricio E. "Investigación acción participativa (IAP). Aspectos conceptuales y dificultades de implementación." *Fundamentos en humanidades*, no. 7–8 (2003): 59–77.

Blundell Jones, Peter, Doina Petrescu and Jeremy Till. *Architecture and Participation*. London and New York: Taylor and Francis, 2005.

Collados, Antonio and Javier Rodrigo. *Transducers: Collective Pedagogies and Spatial Politics*. Granada: Centro José Guerrero, 2010.

Crysler, C. Greig. "The Paradoxes of Design Activism: Expertise, Scale and Exchange". *Field – A Journal of Socially Engaged Art Criticism* (2015): 77–124.

Goodman, Robert. *After the Planners*. New York: Simon and Schuster, 1972.

Hirst, Paul. "Education and the Production of New Ideas". *AA Files*, no. 29 (1995): 44–49.

Hofmann, Susanne. *Architecture is Participation. Die Baupiloten Methods and Projects*. Berlin: Jovis, 2014.

Holub, Barbara and Christine Hohenbüchler (eds.). *Planning Unplanned. Towards a New Function of Art in Society*. Manchester: Cornerhouse Publications, 2015.

Jenkins, Paul and Leslie Forsyth. *Architecture, Participation and Society*. London and New York: Routledge, 2010.

Latour, Bruno. *Reassembling the Social. An Introduction to Actor-Network-Theory*. Oxford: Oxford University Press, 2005.

Ledwith, Margaret and Jane Springett. *Participatory Practice: Community-based Action for Transformative Change*. Bristol: The Policy Press, 2010.

Lefebvre, Henri. *The Production of Space*. Cambridge: Blackwell, 1999 [1976].
Pallasmaa, Juhani. *The Thinking Hand*. New York: John Wiley Sons Inc, 2009.
Sargi, Bechara. *La Participation a l'Être dans la philosophie de Louis Lavelle*. París: Beauchesne et ses fils, 1957.
Sennett, Richard. "The Public Realm". In *The Blackwell City Reader*, edited by Gary Bridge and Sophie Watson, 261–272. Oxford: Wiley-Blackwell, 2010.
Skolimowski, Henryk. *The Participatory Mind: A New Theory of Knowledge and of the Universe*. New York: Penguin Books, 1994.
Yaneva, Albena. *Mapping Controversies in Architecture*. Farnham: Ashgate Publishing Ltd., 2012.

Notes

1. The following projects from the Vallès School of Architecture (ETSAV) have been awarded prizes at Solar Decathlon: LOW3 Building–ETSAV-UPC by Solar Decathlon Europe Award (2010); RESSÒ Building–ETSAV-UPC by Solar Decathlon Europe Award (2014) and ECO Building–ETSAV-UPC by Solar Decathlon Europe Award (2016).
2. In early 2021, the Master's Degree in Architecture has been selected and exhibited amongst ten academic projects for the international exhibition *Human Scale Remeasured: New spatial requirements, societal demands and economic values in Architecture*. The event has been curated by ANCB The Aedes Metropolitan Laboratory in Berlin from January 16, 2021 to May 13, 2021 at the Aedes Architecture Forum.
3. For further information see Paul Jenkins and Leslie Forsyth, *Architecture, Participation and Society* (London and New York: Routledge, 2010); and also Peter Blundell Jones et al., *Architecture and Participation* (London and New York: Taylor and Francis, 2005).
4. Excerpt from Spanish Royal Decree 1892/2008, which regulates the conditions for access to official university degree courses and administration procedures to Spanish public universities. BOE, 11/24/2008, number 238.
5. Margaret Ledwith and Jane Springett, *Participatory practice: Community-based action for transformative change* (Bristol: Policy Press, 2010).
6. Richard Sennett, "The Public Realm" in *The Blackwell City Reader*, ed. Gary Bridge and Sophie Watson (Oxford: Wiley-Blackwell, 2010), 261–272.
7. Barbara Holub and Christine Hohenbüchler (eds.), *Planning Unplanned. Towards a New Function of Art in Society* (Manchester: Cornerhouse Publications, 2015).
8. Bechara Sargi, *La Participation a l'Être dans la philosophie de Louis Lavelle* (Paris: Beauchesne et ses fils, 1957).
9. Bruno Latour, *Reassembling the Social. An Introduction to Actor-Network-Theory* (Oxford: Oxford University Press, 2005).
10. Albena Yaneva, *Mapping Controversies in Architecture* (Farnham: Ashgate Publishing Ltd., 2012), 40.
11. Margaret Ledwith and Jane Springett, *Participatory Practice: Community-based Action for Transformative Change* (Bristol: Policy Press, 2009).

12 Fabricio E. Balcazar, "Investigación acción participativa (IAP). Aspectos conceptuales y dificultades de implementación", *Fundamentos en humanidades*, no. 7–8 (2003): 59–77.
13 Susanne Hofmann, *Architecture is Participation. Die Baupiloten Methods and Projects* (Berlin: Jovis, 2014).
14 Antonio Collados and Javier Rodrigo, *Transducers: Collective Pedagogies and Spatial Politics* (Granada: Centro José Guerrero, 2010).
15 Henryk Skolimowski, *The Participatory Mind: A New Theory of Knowledge and of the Universe* (New York: Penguin Books, 1994).
16 Juhani Pallasmaa, *The Thinking Hand* (New York: John Wiley Sons Inc, 2009).
17 For further information see "OASI" Young Talent Architecture Award, accessed October 27, 2021, http://ytaa.miesbcn.com/work/1106
18 For further information visit "Cardona" Master universitario en Arquitectura, accessed October 8, 2021, https://marq.etsav.masters.upc.edu/es/shared/cardona
19 C. Greig Crysler, "The Paradoxes of Design Activism: Expertise, Scale and Exchange", *Field – A Journal of Socially Engaged Art Criticism* (2015): 77–124, http://field-journal.com/issue-2/crysler
20 Henri Lefebvre, *The Production of Space* (Cambridge: Blackwell, 1999 [1976]).
21 From "Online Etymology Dictionary", accessed October 8, 2021, https://www.etymonline.com/
22 Paul Hirst, "Education and the Production of New Ideas", *AA Files*, no. 29 (1995): 44–49.
23 Robert Goodman, *After the Planners* (New York: Simon and Schuster, 1972).

5 Community-Engaged Architectural Design Learning as Critical Spatial Practice

The Case of the Solidary Mobile Housing Project

Aurelie De Smet, Burak Pak, Yves Schoonjans, Sara Vantournhout, Geraldine Bruyneel, Tineke Van Heesvelde, and Ken De Cooman

Introduction

In this chapter, we discuss the potentials and challenges of facilitating community-engaged experiential learning in architectural design to serve societal needs. Reflecting on experiences and findings from ongoing experiments led by the authors from the KU Leuven Faculty of Architecture in Brussels, Belgium, we elaborate on how Community-engaged Architectural Design Learning (CEADL) can be conceived and implemented as an inclusive *Critical Spatial Practice* (CSP). Service learning is an experiential learning method that allows students to engage meaningfully and together with the community as part of their credit courses.[1] CSPs alter existing practices and established protocols through innovative interventions. This involves inventing new modes of collaboration and *crossbenching*, blurring formal, or disciplinary boundaries while adopting a situated and relational approach.[2]

We will start with a brief introduction to the Solidary Mobile Housing (SMH) research project and an explanation of how teaching and learning were addressed in this context. In the next part, by analysing a series of established modes of collaboration between academia, practice, and society, we will construct a theoretical framework positioning CEADL at the intersection of these three spheres. We will then use this framework to re-examine the SMH project critically. Finally, we will draw conclusions on how, in this case, CEADL cultivated CSP. To conclude, we will highlight the challenges encountered in this venture and reveal potential future directions for bringing practice, academia, and society together to co-create socially and spatially innovative products and services in a sustainable and continuous manner.

The Solidary Mobile Housing Research Project

Since 2016, a wide range of partners from academia, practice, and society have collaborated in the SMH research project. The project aims to develop, test, and refine a model for increasing urban resilience through the co-creation and co-management of mobile houses for houseless people on urban waiting spaces in Brussels. Urban waiting spaces are built or unbuilt, public or private sites, that have been abandoned by a previous use(r) and for which either a future function still has to be determined or for which the installation/realisation of an already defined future function is being delayed for a particular reason.[3] The main research questions of the SMH projects are: *'How can vacant urban areas be temporarily used as sites for housing?'* and *'How can we co-create (intermediate) housing with and for the houseless in Brussels?'*.

The main participants in the SMH project are, first and foremost, eight end-users. They are houseless people from Brussels and the future inhabitants of the project. Directly surrounding them are the architect-researchers, teachers, and students of the KU Leuven Faculty of Architecture and employees of *Centrum Algemeen Welzijnswerk* and *Samenlevingsopbouw Brussel*, two non-profit organisations working on individual wellbeing and neighbourhood work, respectively. Surrounding those are other operational actors such as the architectural firm BC architects, the social construction company Casablanco (involved in the design and construction of the SMH prototype), the NPO *Atelier Groot Eiland* (working on professional insertion), and the Brussels municipality of Jette (where the project is currently being built). Finally, it is also important to mention the sporadically involved actors such as the residents of the immediate surroundings of the site in Jette, the neighbourhood organisations, and the local and sub-local authorities.

Together, these project partners have been developing the SMH project through participatory action research (PAR) in a living lab environment, a community-embedded and community-engaged mode of

Community-Engaged Architectural Design Learning 85

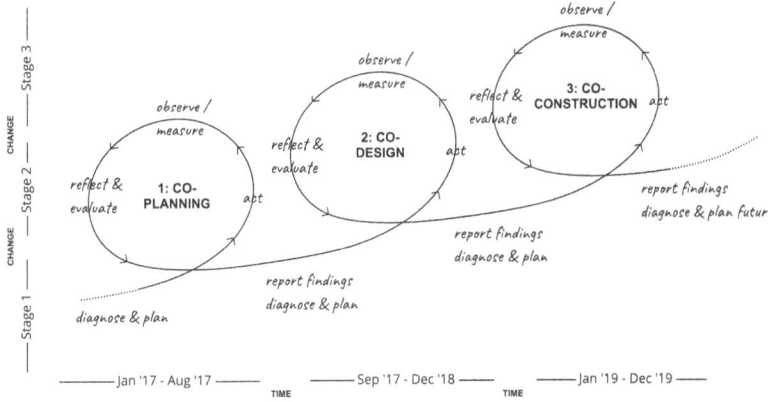

Figure 5.1 SMH Participatory Action Research Cycles 2017–2019
Image by the authors.

research aiming to understand the world by changing it.[4,5] Between 2017 and 2019, three big action research cycles took place: co-planning, co-design and co-development, and dissemination (Figure 5.1). In each cycle, one or more participatory workshops or events were organised to bring the different stakeholders together and collectively construct knowledge. These actions took various forms, such as study trips and site visits, a design studio, co-construction sessions and workshops, and brainstorming, reflection, and evaluation sessions.

The *raison d'être* of the SMH Living Lab was thus to create a collective learning environment involving all the partners, including the houseless, throughout the entire research, and innovation process (Figure 5.2).

The hypotheses behind the SMH project are: (1) by collectively taking part in every step of the conceptualisation, construction, and later in the exploitation of their own houses, the houseless people (end-users) are empowered to participate in the co-creation of their own individual housing units (2) through the employed co-creation methods, the houseless will gradually build a solidary living community, in interactions with the surrounding neighbourhood, and (3) through this process, the houseless people can regain control over, not only on their own housing situation but also on their whole life.

Figure 5.2 Impressions of the SMH co-creation process
Photos by the authors.

The Solidary Mobile Housing Co-creation Model Integrated with Architectural Design Service Learning

After four years of collaboration, the SMH partners have developed a housing co-creation model, the SMH Model (SMH/M), as the project's main results. On the one hand, this model entails a comprehensive set of contributions, including methods and tools for social guidance, skill-building, neighbourhood integration, and university collaboration (through CEADL), combined with strategies for temporary use negotiation and operation in the existing legal framework and for integration in the current Brussels planning and governance codes. On the other hand, the SMH/M also includes design products and technologies for civic empowerment, embodied in a constructed architectural design prototype (Figure 5.3).

Currently, the first SMH pilot project is being realised on an urban waiting space in the municipality of Jette (Brussels, Belgium). This socially situated spatial intervention consists of eight individual housing units and a collective space (Figure 5.4).

Community-Engaged Architectural Design Learning 87

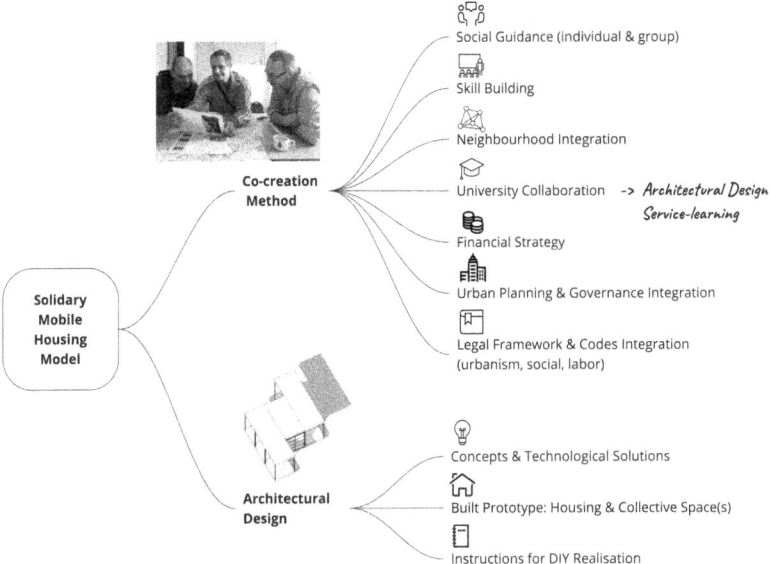

Figure 5.3 Schematic representation of the SMH/M
Image by the authors.

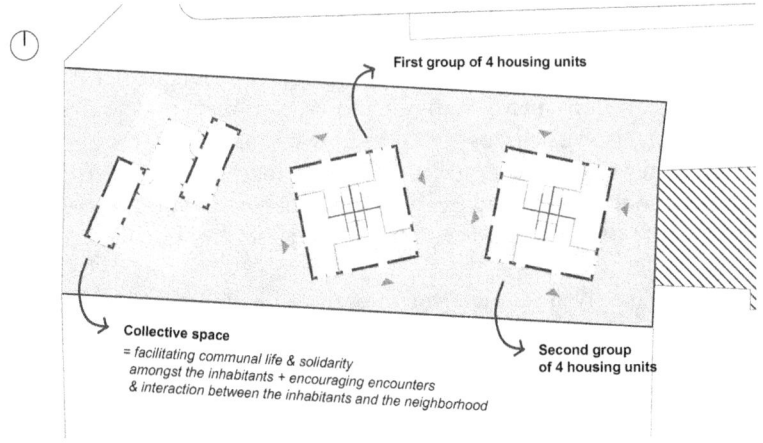

Figure 5.4 Configuration of the SMH project in Jette, Brussels, Belgium
Image by the authors.

Teaching and Learning Embedded in the SMH Project

From 2017 until today (the first semester of the academic year 2019–2020), a CEADL track has been designed and implemented in the context of the SHM project at the KU Leuven Faculty of Architecture. This initiative included four architect-teachers (one actively practising) and more than 30 master's students in the SMH project, allowing them to co-create with future inhabitants under the guidance of two NGOs.

Institutionalised at the KU Leuven since 2016, service-learning is an experiential learning method that allows students to engage in and work together with the community as part of their credit courses. Inspired by both John Dewey's experiential education and Paulo Freire's critical pedagogy known as *educação popular*, service-learning requires students to critically reflect upon their praxis to develop an emerging critical consciousness of self, other, and world.[6,7] Within this context, CEADL is a specific form of research-driven service-learning, involving community-engaged, collaborative research and design, addressing community-identified needs, validating community knowledge, and aiming to contribute to social change.[8]

An essential element of the SMH project is the engagement of the potential end-users and civil society organisations in CEADL courses parallel to the three co-creation phases, starting with the co-planning phase. This process began with an elective course titled 'Urban Projects, Collective Spaces and Local Identities' in the spring semester of 2017. For 14 weeks, 15 students worked together with the project partners to write the architectural design brief (through needs and requirements analysis and case studies) and to develop a temporary use site discovery and selection method (through the development of location scenarios). At this stage, the materials created by the students were used by the social partners to start up conversations with potential end-user candidates at several homeless shelters in Brussels.

Research-driven service-learning embedded in the SMH project continued in the fall semester of 2017. During the co-design phase, a service-learning design studio course was organised. For 14 weeks, 17 students worked together with the civil society organisations, the future inhabitants, three architect-teachers, and a professional architect. In addition to these, several external experts shared knowledge and feedback, forming a service-learning community to co-create preliminary design concepts for the housing units, collective space(s), and the (semi-)public landscape. On a monthly basis, a participatory workshop was organised on the studio day, during which the proposals were presented to the whole team and the external actors to reflect on and improve the design alternatives.

Architect students were included in the SMH project a third time through a service-learning elective course organised by the building construction group in the spring semester of 2018. This elective was a 14-week service-learning course, organised in the spirit of an architectural design office. The professional architect led a team of four students to work on further detailing the final design. They consulted with the project researcher and professors of the Faculty of Architecture involved in the project on a weekly basis to work together on resolving any encountered questions or challenges. Again, the project progress was discussed on monthly basis with the other partners, including the future inhabitants. At the end of this course, a public event was organised to receive input from the projects advisory board members, as well as from other external stakeholders.

The last student engagement took place through yet another elective course titled 'Altering Practices for Urban Inclusion' in the spring semester of 2020. This service-learning course coincided with the co-development and dissemination phase of the project. A group of 13 students worked on initiating neighbourhood interactions and integration through temporary on-site public interventions. The students made several case studies of similar initiatives, reflected collectively on the past co-creation process, developed potential longer-term development ideas, and conducted a critical review of the positioning of the SMH project.

A Conceptual Framework for Architectural Design Service-Learning

As mentioned in the introduction, the overarching aim of this chapter is to understand how CEADL activated socio-spatial modes of collaboration in the case of the SMH project by bringing academia, practice, and society together. To address this question, we will first present a short epistemological discussion followed by a conceptual framework for CEADL. The SMH project will then be critically scrutinised using this framework, focusing on the methods and tools used to enable transdisciplinary collaboration and CEADL.

To explain the conceptual framework for CEADL, it is necessary to touch upon the epistemological basis of knowledge production foreseen in this type of learning. CEADL is based on an approach to knowledge production introduced around the end of the 20th century known as 'Mode 2'. Gibbons et al. described Mode 2 as a new trend in how (scientific) knowledge is produced, in which a multitude of actors from different disciplines and backgrounds focus on problems, projects, or programmes taking place more directly in the context of application or use.[9] As opposed to Mode 1 traditional scientific knowledge production – in which researchers were all too often seen as detached from reality – Mode 2 knowledge production needs to recognise reality, as an always open, complex, networked, and dynamic environment. Mode 2 practices must consider that *'action is never the realization, nor the implementation, of a plan, but the exploration of the unintended consequences of a provisional and revisable version of a project'*.[10] Therefore, Mode 2 knowledge production is, as Latour expresses it, about moving *'from science to research, from objects to projects, and from implementation to experimentation'*.[11]

Subsequently, Carayannis and Campbell further extended the discussion to Mode 3 knowledge production through systems consisting of 'Innovation Networks' and 'Knowledge Clusters'. According to them, Mode 3 involves a *'multilayered, multimodal, and multilateral system encompassing mutually complementary and reinforcing innovation networks and knowledge clusters'*.[12] To realise such a network and cope with the high complexity of reality and formulate efficient answers to the contemporary challenges, academia, practice, and society must collaborate dynamically and structurally with each other. This is also reflected in the Service-learning Model integrating Mode 2 and Mode 3, which situates service-learning, and consequently CEADL, at the intersection of academic study, practical experience, and civic engagement (Figure 5.5).

Today, collaboration amongst at least two of the domains introduced in Figure 5.5 is no longer exceptional. However, knowledge production encompassing all three is still less common due to the abovementioned challenges and complexities. The CEADL framework employs three modes of collaboration for bridging between these domains:

- Participatory design: bringing together practice and society.
- Reflective practice: bringing together practice and academia.
- Living labs: bringing together academia and society.

In the following part, we will discuss the SMH project and illustrate how, in this case, CEADL brought together socio-spatial modes of

Community-Engaged Architectural Design Learning

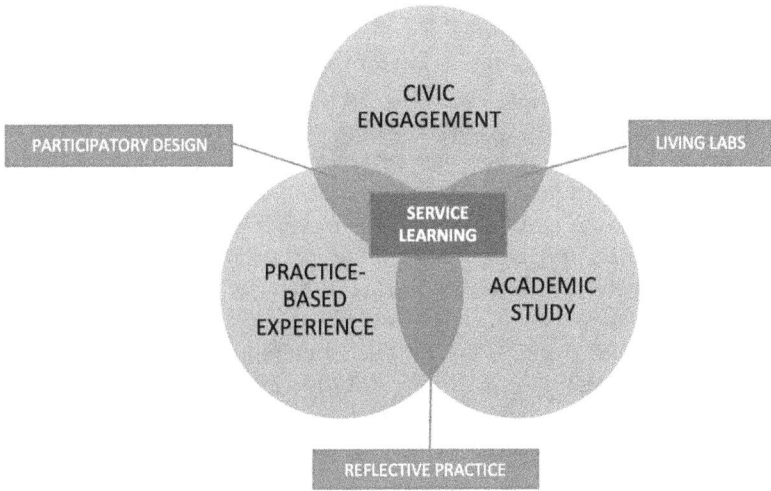

Figure 5.5 The CEADL-framework, extending the Service-learning Model
Image by the authors.

practice, academia, and society through a transformative combination of these three modes of collaboration.

Service-learning Participatory Design

Participatory design is a mode of collaboration bringing together practice and society, which arose in Scandinavia in the sixties and seventies. The approach – at that time, often themed 'cooperative design' – was rooted in work with trade unions aimed at involving workers in improving their work situation. Today participatory design is applied in various disciplines to actively involve all stakeholders in a design process to ensure that the designed product would meet the stakeholder's needs and could be used by them. What is essential is that end-users are seen as the experts of their own experiences in the context of participatory design.[13] In the context of CEADL, engaging end-users in the community-engaged architectural design practices inevitably required participatory modes of design and collaboration. Participatory design was thus an essential collaboration mode for bridging the society and design practices and a vital competence and skill for architecture students to learn.

The Relevance of Reflective Practice

Reflective practice is a mode of collaboration bringing together academia and practice. It is about developing the ability to reflect on one's actions to engage in a process of continuous learning. This concept is central to the work of Donald Schön, who pointed out *'the crisis in the professions, often represented by the perceived gap between formal theory and actual practice'*.[14] Reflective practice involves *'paying critical attention to the practical values and theories which inform everyday actions, by examining practice in a reflective and reflexive way'*.[15] The central idea behind reflective practice is that experience alone does not necessarily lead to learning but that deliberate reflection on experience is essential for learning.[16] As CEADL is inherently practice based, the students participating in this were not only required to learn how to apply professional skills but also how to reflect on their experiences as a way to improve their practice constantly.

The Living Lab as a Learning Environment

In literature, it is possible to find various approaches to living labs. Different researchers have described this concept from different perspectives, such as a network, a platform, a context, a method, an interface, or a system.[17, 18, 19] Specific for living labs is that products and services are tested and developed in their natural environment and interaction with end-users is a prerequisite. As a result, the methods used in living labs are iterative, allowing the knowledge to grow through step-by-step interactions *'between phases and people with diverse competences and perspectives'*.[20] In the context of CEADL, where students need to get involved in incremental, multi-, and transdisciplinary knowledge construction, it is therefore essential that they learn how to foster innovation and develop environments for continuous and systematic experimentation and feedback collection.

Critical Re-Examination of the SMH Project

The SMH 'Live Project' as a Specific Type of Living Lab

In the framework of the SMH project, we organised the different CEADL courses mentioned above as testing grounds for phenomena, methods, and tools. Our approach is based on architectural pedagogy's 'live project' approach. In contrast with academic design studios, live projects occur in a concrete setting, with actors and concrete

Community-Engaged Architectural Design Learning 93

societal issues. In this context, the SMH project included the staging of reorganised relationships, allowing not only the students, teachers, and researchers but also several architectural and social practitioners and the end-users, to participate in the research and teaching activities. This was addressed through careful consideration of the strategies and materials used to facilitate the participation of all the actors in the entire research and co-creation process. In this context, the openness of the PAR as a structuring meta-method also enabled us to use different approaches, methods, strategies, and tools. These came from the domains of architecture and beyond, including ones from social sciences, as well as more artistic and newly constructed ones, adapted to the specific goals and demands of each of the stages of the research and development process. As a result, these helped to develop not only the architectural students' skills and talents but also those of all the other participants. This can be illustrated through the following quotes from the end-users, students, and social workers recorded during the exchange sessions:

> *"The collaboration with different organisations has given me many new insights. Also, with the larger student group, I was able to learn a lot. The fact that there were students of different nationalities involved, brought new insights (for example from people who are used to live in a different climate), which also allowed us the think more broadly about certain issues." (SMH Future Inhabitant)*[21]
>
> *"It was really thought provoking to see what aspects are important and in what ways, even by small interventions, we can make improvements for the settling and integration of these people into the community." (KU Leuven Faculty of Architecture Student)*[22]
>
> *"We are learning a lot from the architects, slowly, by working together and exchanging a lot we are creating a common language and understanding." (Tineke, social worker at Samenlevingsopbouw Brussel)*[23]

As such, the SMH Live Project is a specific, transformative type of living lab, bringing together research, and society and teaching and practice.

From Reflective Practice to Critical Spatial Practice and Crossbenching

Another specificity of the SMH project is that all the partners were always closely involved in a transdisciplinary and trans-sectoral mode of working and reflection, extending Schön's definitions of *reflection-in-action* and *reflecting-on-action* towards socially innovative modes of design. The inclusive incrementality of the PAR process with three co-creation phases was central for enabling continuous reflection. In this way, the participants were encouraged to act as what Markus Miessen is describing as the *'crossbench practitioner'*: an *'outsider and a participator who is not limited by existing protocols, and who enters the arena with creative intellect and the will to generate change'*. The three collaboration modalities of the CEADL framework enabled the creation of a community of practice cultivating crossbenching and pushing the members of this community to go off autopilot and leave the boundaries of what is known to establish new protocols through practice.[24] In the context of the SMH project, this was facilitated, for example, by not letting the rhythm of academia and the research project dictate all actions but also adjusting to the pace of the reality on the terrain and the everyday life of the inhabitants involved. Starting from this, setting up clear protocols for collaboration and a transparent communication structure, involving regular team and partner meetings and intermediate self-evaluation sessions, were quintessential methods and practices for streamlining the co-creation. As a result, all the involved actors were triggered to critically address and rethink their respective fields' established protocols and codes of conduct. In this way, we managed to combine a critical re-thinking of all the involved disciplines with the production of a new body of recognisable work. This is apparent in the following quotes:

> "By very actively building partnerships for the project, we have been able to bring together all the necessary expertise, which is very interesting, everyone learns from everyone, everyone also partly crawls into the role of the other partners. In a certain way and at times everyone becomes an architect, a researcher, a community worker, a participant.... We all learn an awful lot." (Geraldine, project leader and employee of Samenlevingsopbouw Brussel)[25]
>
> "During our studies we learn how to design a space, how to construct a stable building and many other things. But unfortunately, we rarely tackle the reality and the difficult role of being a social architect, someone who cares for the future inhabitants, works with them in a participatory process and finds solutions, again and again, to face the economic reality. I was personally challenged by this project. I'm convinced we need to search for another model, a new model. We need to assure that architectural services are affordable as the ones who really need us, cannot afford us today." (KU Leuven Faculty of Architecture Student)[26]

"This project has also taught me that sometimes we can expect more from our target group: we constantly underestimate them, keeping them unconsciously small. Maybe we can raise the bar a little higher. Of course, we also need sufficient intensive support in return. The height of the bar is proportional to the intensity of the guidance." (Bob, director at Centrum voor Algemeen Welzijnswerk)[27]

"What I also look forward to is giving feedback to new projects. From our experiences we will be able to give real advice on what we should do the same or what can be done differently." (SMH Future Inhabitant)[28]

Through these crossbenching practices, the SMH project thus transforms spatial practices towards involving other societal actors, who previously would have been considered as uninvolved, non-professional outsiders. Crucial to this was the understanding that all partners are equally important and can all make valuable contributions to the co-creation and learning processes.

From Participatory Design to Participation in and through Design

The SMH project revolved around two types of participation and engagement: participation *in* and participation *through* design.[29] On the one hand, participation *in the design process* focused on design-before-use through the design of methods, media, and tools for facilitating participation during the co-creation of the design. In the SMH project, this was addressed through a plethora of methods and tools, such as: user inquiries, participatory site and study visits, participatory hands-on workshops, and participatory review and evaluation sessions. On the other hand, in the participation *through the design product* approach, the architecture itself is seen as an infrastructure for participation, empowering the users to make and remake their own living environments. This approach motivated all participants to rethink architecture as an ever-changing, incomplete, and open infrastructure and focuses on design-in-use such as adaptation, appropriation, tailoring, and redesign.[30] Following this principle of participation through design, we co-created a system of modular building elements consisting of a multifunctional unit, a technical unit, and interchangeable façade panels and re-usable internal wall elements (Figure 5.6).

Through a series of workshops, we are planning for the future users to learn how to assemble and disassemble these elements so that they can combine them to generate an almost endless number of open-plan layouts.

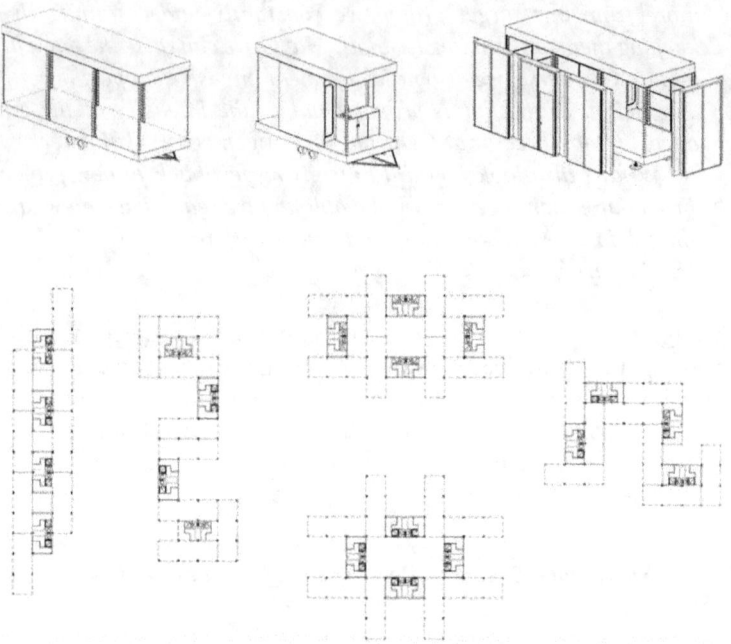

Figure 5.6 The SMH modular elements (multifunctional unit – technical unit – wall panels) and examples of possible architectural configurations using those

Images by the authors.

As a result, the SMH participation *in* and *through* design approach allows participatory design to transcend the conception phase by empowering the users to make and remake their homes, not only during the design process but also after the completion of the project. As such, this approach is transforming participatory design also to include teaching and learning opportunities.

Conclusions

Through the examination of the SMH project presented above, it becomes clear how the transformational approach of the SMH case used CEADL to bring together socio-spatial modes of practice, academia, and society, transforming participatory design, living labs, and reflective practice into participation *in* and *through* design, a live project

Community-Engaged Architectural Design Learning 97

approach and crossbenching practices. In this conclusion, we want to highlight how this fosters CSP.

CSP – which can be defined as a transformative form of critical thinking on and acting in space – is a notion which Jane Rendell and Markus Miessen have introduced.

For Rendell, CSP involves a move from considering architecture and design as objects in space, towards a self-reflective architectural and artistic mode, *'seeking to question and to transform the social conditions of the sites into which they intervene'*. According to Rendell, this approach has three specific qualities: the critical, the spatial, and the interdisciplinary, and is operating *'at a triple crossroads: between theory and practice, between public and private, and between art and architecture'*. With the notion of 'the critical' Rendell refers explicitly to 'critical practices' which, according to her, are dealing with *'social critique, self-reflection, and social change'*.[31, 32]

For Miessen, too, CSP is also about transgressing the borders of architecture as *'a clearly distinguishable field of operation'*. Starting from his observation that there is an urgent need for an *'inversion of participation'*, as this is currently threatened by the *'dangers of consensus, whereby the unfocused canvasing of opinion becomes a shield against taking responsibility or stating a clear direction'*, he is forwarding CSP as a way of criticising the existing normative discourses and frameworks through practice. In this way, he advocates for *'a form of production-as-research'*, which allows *'to test certain ideas, assumptions, and concepts against contemporary reality, different practices and disciplines'*.[33,34]

Critical Spatial Practice (CSP) in the SMH Project

While elaborating on the SMH project from the lens of CSP, we can first say that one of the main aims of the SMH project is to illustrate that 'an alternative is possible', by using a PAR approach to, collectively and incrementally, formulate answers to the research questions, testing these out in practice and adjusting them if needed before moving on. This is in line with Miessen's notion of *'production-as-research'*. In this context, the SMH project formulates a social critique and aims for social change. Moreover, as mentioned in the analysis of the methods and tools used to enable transdisciplinary collaboration and CEADL, self-evaluation and reflection are also integral parts of the project. Together, these elements constitute what Rendell is denoting as *'the critical'*.

Second, when looking at the project partners, it is clear that the SMH project is an 'interdisciplinary' project, another quality of CSP outlined by Rendell. In this context, the quotes presented in the analysis also illustrate how the SMH project is motivating all participants to come out of their comfort zone, switch off the 'autopilot' and critically rethink their role, knowledge, and actions.

Third, the process of co-designing temporary housing on urban waiting spaces also brought to light the underlying controversies, patterns, and (political) values of these spaces and opened discussion on 'the right to the city', not only between the participants but also with external actors. This aligns with Miessen's call to '*carve out an alternative space for collision*' and consciously implement '*zones of conflict*'.[35]

From the above, it is evident that many of the characteristics of CSP outlined by Miessen and the three specific qualities of CSP outlined by Rendell (the critical, the spatial, and the interdisciplinary) are indeed apparent in the SMH project. Moreover, the project is indeed situated at the crossroads: between theory and practice (bringing together a variety of actors from different fields and sectors as well as end-users), between public and private (opening discussions about how to co-create individual housing, collective spaces and (semi-)public co-uses on urban waiting spaces), and between art, architecture, and social work (borrowing methods and tools from each of these fields as well as developing new, transdisciplinary ones).

Reflections on Community-engaged Architectural Design Learning as Critical Spatial Practice

According to Miessen, to adopt a CSP approach (future), architects need to critically re-assess the established codes of conduct of their field and develop new protocols through practice.[36] We believe that this is precisely what architectural education should help students to do. In what follows, we will therefore highlight how we addressed this in the SMH CEADL approach.

First, the SMH CEADL approach allowed us to see teaching and research as practice. Traditionally, architectural courses are monodisciplinary and predominantly teacher and student centred. In light of the realisation of our society's growing complexity and the fact that design and planning can contribute to conditions of justice and injustice, this needs to be rethought and redefined. In the context of the CEADL courses organised in the framework of the SMH project, we intended to move away from traditional models of pedagogical authority and sought to develop a conceptual practice determined by

Community-Engaged Architectural Design Learning 99

the networked relationships of coordinating agents.[37] In this context, we staged reorganised relationships by inviting the social workers and end-users as co-teachers and co-creators to the courses. And we motivated and facilitated the interaction between the students and others within and out of the faculty. The aim was to enable knowledge exchange in practice by establishing an open system of interconnected people and things. This allowed the students to contribute to other fields of knowledge, professions, or discourses from the point of view of 'space'. Using their spatial design capacity, they addressed a real-world problem. Moreover, by contributing to the analysis, planning, and design of affordable housing solutions, they created a significant positive impact on society. It is important to note that such practices not only help to train students to become competent professionals aware of their social role but contribute to the formation of these young people while empowering the future inhabitants and the civil society organisations (as is apparent in the quotes presented in the analysis).

Second, as we already mentioned above, in the context of the SMH project, we noticed how co-designing temporary housing on urban waiting spaces transformed the social conditions of the sites. The SMH CEADL activities (including the public presentations and exhibitions organised in this context) turned waiting spaces into spaces of negotiation, allowing alternative actors to take centre stage and new (power) relations and new ways of engagement to arise.[38] In this sense, through their design proposals, the students are implementing *'zones of conflict'* and fostering micro-political participation in the production of space.

Third, from what was raised in the previous point, it also becomes clear that the CEADL approach is forwarding the 'agency of the artefact' because working on the physical project brings all these different partners from academia, practice, and society together. This puts forward the notion of Spatial Agency, introduced by Jeremy Till as *'another way of doing Architecture'*.[39] In this way, the SMH project is reframing the role(s) of the architect, as well as that of the other actors involved. One of the most critical roles of the architects in CEADL is the facilitation and infrastructuring of the co-creation framework. As a result, the organisation of CEADL requires an engaged attitude and the application of various strategies and methods for *interfacing* between the participants. This also includes providing learning tools for the students, allowing them to establish a relationship with the context, and organising regular self-reflection to make sure everyone is still involved.

Challenges and Future Directions

As this CEADL is an emerging practice, the challenges are still significant. They range from practical and financial (such as having to deal with legal responsibilities and finding funding to build) to disciplinary and institutional (such as having to develop a common vocabulary and a shared understanding of notions such as social inclusion and spatial quality) to ethical (such as dealing with openness and the inclusion of vulnerable users). Other significant challenges are also present in CEADL. For instance, participatory design, reflective practice, and living labs are usually concepts alien to the students, since traditional modes of architectural design education exclude such practices. These challenges also require all the participants to leave the safe zone of the well-known. From a positive perspective, the challenges discussed in this paper can be considered the strength of CEADL for teaching and learning competencies and skills embedded in and relevant to actuality.

To keep on bringing together socio-spatial modes of practice, academia, and society more durably and continuously in the future, potential future directions for academia might be to focus on deepening the understanding of 'research and teaching as practice', through further developing the notion of CEADL. For practice, this might be to allow a reframing of the role of professionals as crossbenching practitioners and co-creators in transdisciplinary and trans-sectoral collaborations. And for society, it might be to keep investing time and effort in participation in and through co-design. CEADL can be improved by constructing novel and more inclusive Mode 3 knowledge production frameworks, innovation networks, and knowledge clusters, which are mutually complementary and reinforcing.

Bibliography

Awan, Nishat, Schneider Tatjana, and Till, Jeremy. *Spatial Agency: Other Ways of Doing Architecture*. London: Routledge, 2013.

Boelens, Luc, Dehaene, Michiel, Goethals, Marleen, Kuhk Annette, and Schreurs, Jan. *Living Labs: co-evolutie planning met onderzoekers, overheden, burgers en ondernemers voor uitvoerbare ruimtelijke projecten*. Brussel: Steunpunt Publicaties, 2015.

Bolton, Gillie. *Reflective Practice: Writing and Professional Development*. London: SAGE Publications, 2010.

Bruno, Latour. "From Multiculturalism to Multinaturalism: What Rules of Method for the New Socio-Scientific Experiments?". *Nature and Culture* 6, no. 1 (2011), 1–17. Accessed October 28, 2021, doi:10.3167/nc.2011.060101.

Carayannis, Elias G., and Campbell, David F.J. *Mode 3 Knowledge Production in Quadruple Helix Innovation Systems*. New York: Springer, 2012.
De Smet Aurelie. "The Role of Temporary Use in Urban (Re)development: Examples from Brussels". *Brussels Studies General Collection*, no. 72 (2013). Accessed October 28, 2021, https://doi.org/10.4000/brussels.1196.
De Smet, Aurelie, Pak, Burak, Schoonjans, Yves, Bruyneel, Geraldine, Van Heesvelde, Tineke, Pincé, Petrus, Van Hoecke, Bob, and De Cooman, Ken. *Final Report of the INNOVIRIS Co-create Project Solidary Mobile Housing, A Real-life Laboratory on the Co-creation of Mobile Housing with Houseless People on Waiting Spaces in the Brussels-Capital Region*. Brussels: KU Leuven Faculty of Architecture, 2020.
Dewey, John. *Experience and Education*. New York: Macmillan, 1963.
Dubé Patrick, Sarrailh, Joëlle, Billebaud, Christophe, Grillet, Claire, Zingraff, Virginie, and Kostecki, Isabelle. *QU'EST-CE QU'UN Living Lab?, LE LIVRE BLANC DES Living Labs*. Montréal: Montréal InVivio, 2014. Accessed October 28, https://www.montreal-invivo.com/wp-content/uploads/2019/12/livre-blanc-ll-umvelt-final-mai-2014.pdf
Fook, Jan. "Reflective Practice and Critical Reflection". In *Handbook for Practice Learning in Social Work and Social Care, Second Edition: Knowledge and Theory*, edited by Joyce Lishman, 363–375. London and Philadelphia: Jessica Kingsley Publishers, 2007.
Freire, Paulo. *Pedagogy of Freedom: Ethics, Democracy, and Civic Courage*. Lanham, MD: Rowman & Littlefield, 1998.
Gibbons, Michael, Limoges, Camille, Nowotny, Helga, Schwartzman, Simon, Scott, Peter and Trow, Martin. *The New Production of Knowledge: The Dynamics of Science and Research in Contemporary Societies*. London: SAGE Publications, 1994.
KU Leuven Service-learning. "What is Service-learning". Accessed October 28, 2021. https://www.kuleuven.be/english/education/sl/whatisservicelearning.
Latour, Bruno. "From Multiculturalism to Multinaturalism: What Rules of Method for the New Socio-Scientific Experiments?". *Nature and Culture* 6, no. 1 (2011), 1–17. Accessed October 28, 2021, doi:10.3167/nc.2011.060101.
Lewin, Kurt. "Frontiers in Group Dynamics: Concept, Method and Reality in Social Science; Equilibrium and Social Change". *Human Relations* 1, no. 1 (1947), 5–41. Accessed October 28, 2021, https://doi.org/10.1177/001872674700100103.
Miessen, Markus. *The Nightmare of Participation (Crossbench Praxis as a Mode of Criticality)*. Berlin: Sternberg Press, 2010.
Miessen, Markus. *Crossbenching: Towards a Proactive Mode of Participation as Critical Spatial Practice*. London: Centre for Research Architecture Goldsmiths College University of London, 2017.
Pak, Burak. "ICT-enabled Bottom-up Architectural Design", *ArchNet – International Journal of Architectural Research* 10, no. 2 (2016), 26–40. Accessed October 28, 2021, doi: 10.26687/archnet-ijar.v10i1.738.

Pak, Burak. "Enabling Bottom-up Practices in Urban and Architectural Design Studios". *Knowledge Cultures* 5, no. 2 (2017), 84–102. Accessed October 28, 2021, doi: 10.22381/KC5220176.

Pak, Burak, De Smet, Aurelie, and Schoonjans, Yves. "Solidary Mobile Housing Live Project". In *WTC Tower Teachings, Reports from One and a Half Years of Nomadic Architecture Education in Brussels*, edited by Boie, G., Boutsen, D, Fens, R., De Maeyer, G., Houttekier, B., Schamelhout, J. Brussel: KU Leuven, Faculty of Architecture, 2019.

Rendell, Jane. *Art and Architecture: A Place Between*. London: Tauris, 2006.

Rendell, Jane. "Critical Spatial Practice". In *Art Incorporated*, edited by Sabine Nielsen and Christine Buhl Andersen. Copenhagen: Kunstmuseet Koge Skitsesamling, 2008.

Robles, Ana G., Hirvikoski, Tuja, Schuurman Dimitri, and Stokes, Lorna. *Introducing ENoLL and Its Living Lab Community*. Brussels: ENoLL, 2015. Accessed October 28, 2021, https://ec.europa.eu/digital-single-market/en/news/introducing-enoll-and-its-living-lab-community.

Sanders, Elizabeth B. and Dandavate, Uday, "Design for Experiencing: New Tools". In *Proceedings of the First International Conference on Design and Emotion*, edited by C.J. Overbeeke and P. Hekkert, 90–94. Delft: TU Delft, 1999.

Schein, Edgar H. *Organizational Culture and Leadership*, 4th ed. San Francisco, CA: Wiley, 2010.

Ståhlbröst, Anna and Holst, Marita. *The Living Lab Methodology Handbook*. Stockholm: Vinnova, 2013. Accessed October 28, 2021, https://www.ltu.se/cms_fs/1.101555!/file/LivingLabsMethodologyBook_web.pdf.

Strand, Kerry J., Cutforth, Nicholas, Stoecker, Marullo, Randy, Sam and Donohue, Patrick. *Community-based Research and Higher Education: Principles and Practices*. San Francisco, CA: Jossey-Bass, 2003.

Notes

1 "What is Service-learning" KU Leuven Service-learning website, accessed October 28, 2021, https://www.kuleuven.be/english/education/sl/whatisservicelearning
2 Markus Miessen, *Crossbenching: Towards a Proactive Mode of Participation as a Critical Spatial Practice* (London: Centre for Research Architecture Goldsmiths College University of London, 2017).
3 Aurelie De Smet "The Role of Temporary Use in Urban (Re)development: Examples from Brussels." *Brussels Studies General collection* 72 (2013), accessed October 28, 2021, https://doi.org/10.4000/brussels.1196.
4 Kurt Lewin, "Frontiers in Group Dynamics: Concept, Method and Reality in Social Science; Equilibrium and Social Change", *Human Relations* 1 no. 1 (1947), 5–41.
5 Edgar H. Schein, *Organizational Culture and Leadership*, 4th ed. (San Francisco, CA: Wiley, 2010).
6 John Dewey, *Experience and Education* (New York: Macmillan, 1963).

7 Paulo Freire, *Pedagogy of Freedom: Ethics, Democracy, and Civic Courage* (Lanham, MD: Rowman & Littlefield, 1998).
8 Kerry J. Strand, Nicholas Cutforth, Randy Stoecker, Sam Marullo and Patrick Donohue, *Community-based Research and Higher Education: Principles and Practices* (San Francisco, CA: Jossey-Bass, 2003).
9 Michael Gibbons, Camille Limoges, Helga Nowotny, Simon Schwartzman, Peter Scott and Martin Trow, *The New Production of Knowledge: The Dynamics of Science and Research in Contemporary Societies* (London: SAGE Publications, 1994).
10 Bruno Latour, "From Multiculturalism to Multinaturalism: What Rules of Method for the New Socio-Scientific Experiments?", *Nature and Culture* 6, no. 1 (2011), 1–17, accessed October 28, 2021, doi:10.3167/nc.2011.060101.
11 Ibid.
12 Elias G. Carayannis, and David F.J. Campbell, *Mode 3 Knowledge Production in Quadruple Helix Innovation Systems* (New York: Springer, 2012).
13 Elizabeth B. Sanders and Uday Dandavate, "Design for Experiencing: New Tools", *Proceedings of the First International Conference on Design and Emotion*, eds. C.J. Overbeeke and P. Hekkert (Delft: TU Delft, 1999), 90–94.
14 Jan Fook, "Reflective Practice and Critical Reflection" *Handbook for Practice Learning in Social Work and Social Care, Second Edition: Knowledge and Theory*, ed. Joyce Lishman (London and Philadelphia: Jessica Kingsley Publishers, 2007), 363–375.
15 Gillie Bolton, *Reflective Practice: Writing and Professional Development* (London: SAGE Publications, 2010).
16 Dewey, *Experience and Education*.
17 Patrick Dubé Joëlle Sarrailh, Christophe Billebaud, Claire Grillet, Virginie Zingraff and Isabelle Kostecki, *QU'EST-CE QU'UN Living Lab?, LE LIVRE BLANC DES Living Labs* (Montréal: Montréal InVivio, 2014), accessed October 28, 2021, https://www.montreal-invivo.com/wp-content/uploads/2019/12/livre-blanc-ll-umvelt-final-mai-2014.pdf.
18 Luc Boelens, Michiel Dehaene, Marleen Goethals, Annette Kuhk and Jan Schreurs, *Living labs: co-evolutie planning met onderzoekers, overheden, burgers en ondernemers voor uitvoerbare ruimtelijke projecten* (Brussel: Steunpunt Publicaties, 2015).
19 Ana G. Robles, Tuja Hirvikoski, Dimitri Schuurman and Lorna Stokes, *Introducing ENoLL and its Living Lab community* (Brussels: ENoLL, 2015), accessed October 28, 2021, https://ec.europa.eu/digital-single-market/en/news/introducing-enoll-and-its-living-lab-community.
20 Anna Ståhlbröst and Marita Holst, *The Living Lab Methodology Handbook* (Stockholm: Vinnova, 2013), accessed October 28, 2021, https://www.ltu.se/cms_fs/1.101555!/file/LivingLabsMethodologyBook_web.pdf.
21 SMH Future Inhabitant, interview with Tineke Van Heesvelde, April, 2020.
22 KU Leuven Faculty of Architecture Student self-written declaration to the authors, April, 2020.
23 Tineke, interview with Aurelie De Smet, January 2018.
24 Markus Miessen, *The Nightmare of Participation (Crossbench Praxis as a Mode of Criticality)* (Berlin: Sternberg Press, 2010).
25 Geraldine, interview with Tineke Van Heesvelde, April, 2020.

26 KU Leuven Faculty of Architecture Student self-written declaration to the authors, April, 2020.
27 Bob, interview with Tineke Van Heesvelde, April, 2020.
28 SMH Future Inhabitant, interview with Tineke Van Heesvelde, April, 2020.
29 Burak Pak, "ICT-enabled Bottom-up Architectural Design" *ArchNet – International Journal of Architectural Research* 10, no. 2 (2016), 26–40, accessed October 28, 2021, doi: 10.26687/archnet-ijar.v10i1.738.
30 Burak Pak, "Enabling Bottom-up Practices in urban and Architectural Design Studios" *Knowledge Cultures* 5, no. 2 (2017), 84–102, accessed October 28, 2021, doi: 10.22381/KC5220176.
31 Jane Rendell, *Art and Architecture: A Place Between* (London: Tauris, 2006).
32 Jane Rendell, "Critical Spatial Practice" in *Art Incorporated*, edited by Sabine Nielsen and Christine Buhl Andersen (Copenhagen: Kunstmuseet Koge Skitsesamling, 2008).
33 Miessen, *Crossbenching*.
34 Miessen, *The Nightmare of Participation*.
35 Miessen, *Crossbenching*.
36 Ibid.
37 Burak Pak, Aurelie De Smet and Yves Schoonjans "Solidary Mobile Housing Live Project" in *WTC Tower Teachings, Reports from One and a Half Years of Nomadic Architecture Education in Brussels*, edited by G. Boie, D. Boutsen, R. Fens, G. De Maeyer, B. Houttekier, and J. Schamelhout (Brussel: KU Leuven, Faculty of Architecture, 2019).
38 Aurelie De Smet, Burak Pak, Yves Schoonjans, Geraldine Bruyneel, Tineke Van Heesvelde, Petrus Pincé, Bob Van Hoecke and Ken De Cooman, *Final Report of the Innoviris Co-create Project Solidary Mobile Housing, A Real-life Laboratory on the Co-creation of Mobile Housing with Houseless People on Waiting Spaces in the Brussels-Capital Region* (Brussels: KU Leuven Faculty of Architecture, 2020).
39 Nishat Awan, Tatjana Schneider and Jeremy Till, *Spatial Agency: Other Ways of Doing Architecture* (London: Routledge, 2013).

6 Co-Creating Urban Strategies through Trans-Local Learning Alliances

Catalina Ortiz

Introduction

Educators have the imperative to unsettle the cannon of what constitutes Urban Design as praxis, whose knowledge counts in city-making practices, and what counts as design. The pandemic made evident the intertwined crisis that we inhabit and how urban spaces amplify the systems of oppression that drive urban processes in cities of the global North and South alike. The pandemic has also become a portal to push for new spatial imaginations and foster spatial justice anew. In this endeavour, the role of urban design education is key to shaping more emancipatory design practices as the discipline has been complicit in the reproduction of spatial injustices. This chapter contends that research-based design, trans-local learning alliances, and critical pedagogy are pivotal for framing urban design as a progressive co-creative process.

I will outline how the MSc on Building and Urban Design in Development (BUDD) within The Bartlett Development Planning Unit (DPU) at University College London (UCL) has approached its "Overseas Practice Engagement" (OPE) during pandemic times, navigating the new challenges brought to postgraduate higher education in the UK and their international collaborators. The collective intellectual project of the MSc on BUDD sits at the intersection of critical urban theory, critical design studies, and southern urban practice. This provides a singular approach to frame experiential learning through engagement with partnerships in Global South cities. Our Master's programme brings together professionals from different disciplinary backgrounds coming from multiple countries in the world. This feature shapes a transdisciplinary approach to our "Overseas Practice Engagement" that takes place during three months as the culmination of the collective learning of a year-long programme.

DOI: 10.4324/9781003267683-7

Over the span of two academic years (2019–2021), we have collaborated remotely with three organisations in the city of Medellin, Colombia, reaching up to 60 participants in each edition of the collaboration. The site of inquiry was the neighbourhood of Moravia, a site that represents urban learning about the multiplicity and potentials of informality and "slum" upgrading programmes. We generated a trans-local alliance among our programme, the Moravia Cultural Development Centre – a public social facility –, Moravia Resiste – a grassroots organisation that advocates for the right to remain in the territory –, and COONVITE – a cooperative of social architecture –. Our driving questions were: How can Moravia's territory in Medellin be framed as living heritage? And consequently, what type of socio-spatial strategies can be imagined responding to urban transformation? We used these questions to shape the digital co-design process we engaged with.

We focus on the living heritage of the place as the departing point to propose multiscale socio-spatial strategies, to improve the neighbourhood and counteract threats of eviction. We delved into the leverage that urban design can provide to change stigmas against the place and connect with others' life stories to catalyse ideas about improving specific aspects of the spatial quality of their collective life. We contribute to the recognition of everyday spatial practices in *barrios populares* – so-called informal settlements – as the living heritage of the city and the agency of Integral Neighborhood Upgrading – also known as slum upgrading – as a path for progressive urban planning and design. Our approach to the OPE served as an interactive setting to expand action-based design skills while contributing to the ongoing grounded work of local community-led organisations.

This chapter is structured in five parts. The first one explains the institutional setting, the curricular location of the "Overseas Practice Engagement" and the premises that underpin this pedagogy. The second part illustrates the "real-world design problem" we addressed, portraying how urban design can contribute to fighting eviction threads by uncovering the local living heritage of our site of inquiry. The third one delves into the trans-local learning alliance as an approach to engage with organisations outside the university while having students and tutors spread in different parts of the globe based on research-based design. The fourth part illustrates how we operationalised the living heritage framework to drive a digital co-design process. The last part reflects the outputs we generated over two consecutive years of collaboration and lessons from designing distributed public engagement.

Setting the Stage: Critical Pedagogy and Curricular Location

Building on The Bartlett Development Planning Unit's long-term tradition, the Overseas Practice Engagement (OPE) epitomises the connections between different communities to enhance learning processes by connecting teaching, research, and "real world" communities.[1] Institutionally the OPE is part of UCL's Connected Curriculum that in pandemic times provided a basis for a consistent digital pedagogy, where students connect with people (peers, teachers, postgraduate teaching assistants, and other online UCL communities), knowledge and research (carefully curated resources), and the wider world. The challenge we faced was to adapt these principles to foster an online learning community engaging with different digital pedagogies. It is not about using digital technologies for teaching but, rather, about approaching these tools from a critical pedagogical perspective. It is as much about using digital tools thoughtfully as it is about deciding when not to use digital tools and about paying attention to the impact of digital tools on learning.[2]

The OPE synthesises the digital hands-on experience of using the skills, concepts, theories, and techniques of urban design for development, taught in the BUDD Modules. This learning experience enables the integration of learning from the different modules during the first terms of the programme. The practice engagements are meant not only to galvanise the linkages between theory and practice, grasp grounded applications of abstract concepts, and develop interpersonal skills but also to be a subject of critical thinking and a sequence of subjective encounters.[3] Therefore, the OPE acts as a fertile arena for new knowledge generation and collaboration through research-based design. It relates to what in the US is called service-learning pedagogy as a space that "provides the necessary space and conceptual tools for students to analyse the narratives of place, self, and others that shape their identities. This, in turn, will encourage them to reflect critically on the discipline".[4]

Since the BUDD programme sits at the intersection of critical urban theory, critical design studies, and southern urban practice, its educational approach is influenced by critical pedagogy. Critical pedagogy is mainly associated with the work of the Brazilian thinker Paulo Freire. His political commitment to work towards a radical democracy emphasised bringing "students' worldview into the educational process"[5] under the premise that "pedagogic practice requires an understanding of the genesis of knowledge itself".[6] He envisioned a public school system "that seeks collective knowledge, by articulating critical, scientific knowledge through world experiences".[7] In this context, the role of pedagogy and politics were intertwined in the search for "a social invention that demands a certain political knowledge, a knowledge born of the struggle for and the reflection on citizenship itself".[8] These ideas inspire our pedagogical approach and the alliances we make to foster reciprocal and meaningful learning processes for all our collaborators.

The role of a critical pedagogy focuses on the cultivation of political subjects to transform the world. The legacy of Freire has inspired educators to work around "dialogue, learning from difference, citizenship, collaboration, historical consciousness, alternative ways of knowing, humility, self-reflexivity, and social justice".[9] He emphasised how the relationship between cognitive-affective learning and theory-practice were "undichotomizable" since "one of the political-pedagogical acts that truly progressive educators and community-based movements need to accomplish is the demonstration that theory cannot be separated from practice".[10] With this impetus, our entire curricula design operates and gives basis to some of our core premises: (a) urban design is part and parcel of the politics of space production, and urban design education is part of the political economy of higher education; (b) urban design needs to become a plural epistemic field to understand city-making practices beyond the western gaze and against the coloniality of city production and university structures; (c) we acknowledge that the ethics of engagement for practice does not occur in a political vacuum as "city dwellers are creators of epistemologies with different ways of knowing, but with differential leverage to influence power structures"[11]; and (d) a recalibration of urban design repertoires is needed to pursue collectively spatial justice based on recognising "popular" practices and knowledge about city-making.

The experience presented in this chapter undertakes research-based design through digital means as it relies on an online learning community. We understand that a learning community involves people who: share goals, interests, and concerns in what they do, bring their personal and professional experiences as well as knowledge to social interaction, and further develop meanings regarding past, ongoing, and future experiences. All this can be achieved through group and individual reflection, collaboration, interaction, support, and building a sense of connectedness in an unlimited physical and temporal space.[12,13] Notwithstanding the sensorial deprivation of the online world and the unevenness of digital literacy and internet access, the exchange of experiences has been meaningful and enriching. We worked remotely; nonetheless, we generated new affective cartographies shaped by the participants' commitment, enthusiasm, and dedication despite their different personal situations and locations.

The BUDD OPE is an experience of knowledge co-production and co-design. It is a pivotal stage of what we call the "the practice module" that runs across three terms during the master program. The guiding question of this module is: How to contribute to fostering translocal spatial justice through urban design? A studio-based pedagogy precedes the OPE to provide students with the opportunity to test theories through practice. The OPE is based on the incremental learning of the module contents. On the one hand, the project is grounded on the research design method learnt in the urban intervention studio, where the comparative urban design approach contributed to uncovering the differential trajectories of spatial transformation, discovering interconnected urban challenges, and dismantling preconceptions about how urban interventions can be shaped. On the other hand, the OPE project aims to build connections with partners and subjects, where the reflexivity of the designer and the sensibilities of human interaction are key.

The Grounding: Fighting Eviction Threads

The BUDD OPE aims at reframing informality as the city's living heritage to reshape neighbourhood upgrading strategies (Figure 6.1). This

Figure 6.1 Moravia Resist is the motto for the right to stay put
Photo: Catalina Ortiz.

approach results from a long-term research engagement with the city of Medellin, its urban policies and politics, its contestations, and its networks of urban actors that shape the public debate around these issues. Medellin has been portrayed in the last decade as a site of innovation in urban governance and a laboratory of local state "best practices" to address in tandem violence and "informality". The Medellin model is underpinned by a focus on strategic planning, urban design, and architecture in traditionally excluded peripheral neighbourhoods. Iconic architecture, mobility infrastructure, and strategic urban projects are used as the linchpin strategy to increase accessibility and generate symbolic inclusion under the banner of "Social Urbanism".[14] The urban intervention strategy has been based on targeting the areas of the city with the highest degrees of deprivation and high crime rates – located in the northeast, central west and central east zones – as well as the potential for expanding the metropolitan centrality in the river corridor in the lowlands of the centre-north. Urban projects rely on urban acupuncture and transit as catalysts for urban transformation to integrate the transit system and its innovative cable cars lines to the urban fabric through the generation of public spaces and the construction of iconic architecture for public facilities.[15]

In this intervention scheme, the neighbourhood of Moravia has been paradigmatic of the so-called Medellin model. That is why Moravia represents a site of urban learning about the multiplicity and potentials of informality. The neighbourhood of Moravia is characterised by its central location within the city of Medellin, its social mobility, its process of spatial transformation and its rich cultural diversity. Moravia is a neighbourhood of migrants that originated due to forced displacements, war violence, and social injustices. In the 1950s and late 1970s, inhabitants started building shelters around and on top of the former garbage dump of the city until it became a "public hazard", resulting in a threatening area for health and safety. As a means of addressing the environmental and social problems of the neighbourhood, in 2020, the State re-establishes its presence in the territory with a proposal of an integral urban intervention: the macro-project of Moravia. The macro-project included seven programmes that considered housing construction and upgrading, public space, tenancy and legal rights, socio-cultural development, strengthening of local economies, and health issues. From 2004 to 2011, a multi-sectoral slum-upgrading urban initiative – known as the Partial Plan of Integral Improvement of Moravia and aligned with the city's "Social Urbanism" policy – was designed and implemented.[16]

Since 2014 the new strategic spatial plan of the city ignited a renewed interest in densifying the central area and the lowlands of the Valley where the city sits. Given the prime real estate location of the neighbourhood and despite the community social organisation and the public investments in the area, it was "re-zoned" as an area of urban renewal. This severe regulation change suggests a tabula rasa approach going against the incremental consolidation that guides "slum" upgrading programmes. This shift has prompted threads of eviction in the already very densified area. The neighbourhood of Moravia is an archetype of the history of many popular neighbourhoods of Medellín: the settlement through informal processes, the configuration of strong bonds of solidarity and forms of social and community organisation, the continued presence of actors in the armed conflict and organised crime, the expulsion and reception of the displaced population, and a historical absence of the State.[17] Rather than romanticise the cultural richness of the place, we seek to grasp the complexities and contradictions of urban transformations to enable a reflection about how to rethink different urban futures for Moravia. We propose using a living heritage approach to respond to those threats. In this quest, we pursue innovating the Integral Neighbourhood Upgrading's agency as a path for progressive urban planning and design.

The Approach: Trans-Local Learning Alliances for Research-Based Design

The broader purpose of the OPE is to deepen the abilities to identify and trigger potential spaces of opportunity towards a just and inclusive socio-spatial transformation. As Sweet et al.[18] suggest, community-based research requires trust, commitment, care, respect, knowledge, and responsibility, the characteristics of the ethic of love. In this quest, rather than teaching "skills" only, the learning goal "is to develop students' critical reflexivity, specifically their understanding of the narratives of people and places that shape their identities and hence their engagements with marginalised and overlooked".[19] In this light, we framed our partnerships using the learning alliance approach[20] as a methodological strategy. This approach conceives the promotion of the interaction of "multiple actors with multi-layered sources of knowledge to cope with the complexity of fostering continuous technological, social and institutional innovations to respond to rapidly changing context and demands".[21] It enables establishing strategic partnerships to increase organisations' adaptive capacity and avenues to facilitate collective knowledge management around a common urban challenge.

In the context of urban studies and planning, Moreno-Leguizamon et al. have argued "that a learning alliance is an innovative methodology that can contribute to multicultural planning by (1) promoting the involvement of new planning stakeholders and the institutionalisation of learning alliance outcomes, (2) ensuring capacity-building strategies, (3) emphasising documentation and dissemination as innovative practices, and (4) strengthening the network capacity of a community".[22] Inspired by this approach, we have adapted its operation not only to the purpose of research-based design but also to our pedagogical work related to comparative urban design[23] with the potential of having students located in several different cities across three continents. The alliance generation occurs through a *pedagogy of experience* where urban experience becomes the source of practices and learnings, remaining close to what educationalists have called "learning by doing". We explore how urban design fosters trans-local urban justice through research-based design learning and generates a spatial understanding of urban inequalities and the potential for transformation in a trans-local fashion.

The notion of trans-locality has gained interest in the last decade, particularly in urban geography. Trans-locality helps us frame the learning across cities and foreground the interdependence of urbanisation processes as immersed in flows and circulations of people, goods, ideas, policies, finance, urban aspirations, etc. Greiner and Sakdapolrak[24] argue that the notion of trans-locality contributes to challenging dichotomous geographical conceptions such as local-global by focusing on non-hierarchic interactions and configurations across scales. Moreover, they contend that "the actor-oriented focus on the social production of trans-locality enhances a more explicit discussion of the temporal dynamics, path dependence and time-space interconnections of socio-spatial dynamics... and the co-production of connectedness by mobile and immobile populations"[25]. I call it a trans-local learning alliance to highlight the joint work of organisations and participants that operate in different locations whose learning and ability to innovate derives not only from their different interests and backgrounds but also from the lived experience of the interconnections and singularities of multiple urban trajectories. Trans-local learning alliance problematises the dichotomic views of global north and south and engages with the patterns or resemblance and singularities that cities across the globe encapsulate.[26]

Co-Creating Urban Strategies 113

Despite being amid the pandemic, our learning alliance between the Moravia Cultural Centre (CDCM), the Moravia Resiste Collective, the Cooperative Coonvite, and the Master on BUDD from DPU, UCL achieved its collaborative work. We understand ourselves as a diaspora that met from the co-presence of the digital space to tackle a common challenge: how to address research-based design to have an impact in the city decision-making process inspired by popular education and critical pedagogy.[27] We agreed to bring participants of different ages to allow an intergenerational learning experience, particularly with the more experienced community leaders and the young generations of inhabitants of the neighbourhood and undergrad students of the city. We had more contingent collaborators and guests to catalyse local and international networks with other relevant stakeholders influencing Medellin's urban development, building from the research project COiNVITE, a Transmedia Storytelling Platform for trans-local learning about neighbourhood upgrading experiences in Medellin.

The alliance focuses on reimagining critical socio-spatial strategies with attention to the ongoing process of urban change of Moravia and the city's contested urban conditions. We agreed on the following driving questions: How can Moravia's territory in Medellin be framed as living heritage? And consequently, what type of socio-spatial strategies can be imagined responding to urban transformation?

The learning alliance acknowledges the diverse objectives that each organisation seeks. With this alliance, the CDCM aims to generate an exchange of experiences in the face of the plurality of memories, as a fundamental component in the construction of identity, especially those that refer to the collective identity, the territory, its forms of occupation, meanings, and struggles. The co-design process's outputs feed into the organisation's cultural agenda. Moravia Resiste aims to defend the socially produced territory of Moravia from the renewal initiatives based on the long-term process of integral neighbourhood upgrading. Moravia Resiste is expanding the public debate about urban development questioning urban development for whom? Their engagement with the learning alliance aims (1) to showcase their spaces of encounter, co-creation, negotiation, and struggles; (2) to exchange lessons from similar international experiences; and (3) to enable dialogue with Moravia's communities leveraging cultural expressions to inform collective strategic action. COONVITE aims to provide a space for architecture students to envision alternative design practices relying on an exchange of experience between popular and academic

114 *Catalina Ortiz*

knowledge. They were interested in exploring how to draw the intangible to document what Moravia means and enable spaces to continue nurturing and expanding the idea of memory for a promising future.[28]

The Work Together: Digital Co-Design of Upgrading Strategies

Our shared aim was uncovering the living heritage of Moravia to leverage it as a tool to counteract eviction threats (Figure 6.2). That is why in the OPE, the trans-local learning alliance strived to innovate neighbourhood upgrading strategies through the lenses of living heritage. The living heritage framework emerged as part of a broader debate on Critical Heritage Studies about the tension between "authorised" and "unauthorised" heritage discourses and practices, which has led to an artificial and oversimplified dichotomisation of the heritage sector.[29] This area of study shifted the meaning of heritage from the idea of a homogeneous single identity toward a polyphony of values and from the idea of authoritative expertise to that of dissonance. The living heritage framework allows us to go in-depth in understanding the place, place-making practices, and culture of the so-called informal community as a starting point to avoid its erasure

Figure 6.2 Affective interactions in the digital co-design process
Source: Atlas of Living Heritage, drawn by Naiara Yumiko.

from demolition by demonstrating its value and advocating for societal recognition.[30,31]

The Research-Based Design Framework

The OPE adapted the living heritage framework to guide our collective work. Poulios[32] implies that through a living heritage approach, a site must be first judged upon the continuity criteria to determine if the living heritage approach is applicable. The approach is based on recognising the role of the community in the care of heritage (i.e., core community); thus, allowing communities to become active political subjects of a broader process of socio-cultural change. As defined by ICCROM, living heritage can be characterised by continuity: continuity of *use* (as a function); continuity of *community connections*; continuity of *cultural expressions* (both tangible and intangible), and continuity of *care* (through traditional or established means). These four axes became the basis for the distribution of teams. However, we transformed and adapted some of their meanings and focus to make them more relevant for guiding the co-design of socio-spatial strategies of neighbourhood upgrading: (a) function or use became *landscapes of recycling* to reflect one of the most singular livelihoods dynamic of the place; (b) community connections was also linked to *social communication* practices to include citizen media and other analogue and digital strategies to link with the public debates; (c) cultural expressions were linked to *memory and migrations* to reflect the constant influx of population and their diverse backgrounds; (d) care in the literature is understood in terms of the maintenance of a site, and we turn it into *systems of care* to extend the care practices of humans and non-humans.

The Preparatory Work and Teams Composition

During 2020 and 2021, around 120 participants were part of this collaborative process, with 60 members active each year. After an extensive preparatory phase, the organising committee with representatives of each partner organisation created a bilingual shared term of reference and a set of ethics of engagement premises to convey the scope and operationalisation of the joint work before the pandemic. Our master students, distributed in over 25 countries, dedicated two months of preparation prior to engaging with partners by devoting time to readings, guest seminars, and workshops to map out the socio-political configurations and the territorial dynamics of the place. In parallel, each organisation selected and updated participants on the terms of reference and the expectation about the learning alliance. As a result of the pandemic, an unexpected area of preparation work became the training on the use of digital tools, particularly for senior community leaders, and at the same time try to address the asymmetries of the digital divide experienced in low-income households making sure community members would have access to digital devices and data. Community partners prepared short videos to illustrate the neighbourhood sites more relevant for each theme to capture the everyday life experience of the space.

The Ethics of Engagement and Care

Developing an ethics of engagement only can be possible if a constant reflexive attitude is embodied. This implies critically examining one's own views, assumptions, and convictions to frame the encounters and devise the spatial implications of life stories. As a result, "the ethics of engagement is not a fixed moral code of conduct, but rather it is (a) a reflexive practice of one's responsibility with others; (b) a constant inter-subjective negotiation on how to guide collective action; (c) a systematic way of framing issues, respecting cultural sensitivities".[33] In pandemic times, we had to change assumptions about people's availability and conditions to contribute to the creative investigative work and bring care to the centre of human relations. We provided a set of protocols to prioritise well-being and mental health protection. This was particularly important in periods where the social unrest in Colombia was very severe, and several participants have experienced loss or ill health.

The Phases of the Digital Encounters

The digital co-design work relied on synchronous sessions and asynchronous activities during the four to five weeks of intense collaboration. Given that participants were spread in different time zones, we decided to have a rhythm of two to three plenary encounters per week, in which we would start framing the scope of the phase, providing guests' thematic inputs and tutorials for each team's work. The co-design process was built as an incremental progression on understanding the challenge and teamwork dynamics to substantiate the proposal of multi-scale socio-spatial strategies. Each team would develop a singular work plan and a distribution of the asynchronous tasks. We proposed five stages, one per week, guided with the following questions:

(a) What will we do and how? (b) What is our design/research question and method? (c) What is our proposed socio-spatial strategy? (d) How to (re)present our socio-spatial strategy? (e) How to synthesise and communicate our strategy to a broader audience? Using incremental and simple phases helped the diversity of participants to navigate the teamwork.

The Closing: Outputs and Distributed Public Engagement

I call for distributed public engagement to design a multi-actor, multi-scale, and multi-channel communication strategy to publicly debate urban intervention approaches and their impacts (Figure 6.3). Since the learning alliance seeks to influence the public debate about the state's spatial intervention for Moravia, the engagement with different publics was pivotal. To demonstrate the cultural richness and contributions of the neighbourhood to the city that a renewal process could erase, in pandemic times, we had to maximise the digital channels and formats – including analogue – that would allow us to reach different audiences. The results of the first year of work were translated into an open-source book and a wiki page that operates as a digital archive of the project. We decided to focus on a research-based design to produce an Atlas of Living Heritage.[34] An Atlas contributes to creating

Figure 6.3 A re-imagined Moravia for the Atlas of Living Heritage
Source: Atlas of Living Heritage, drawn by Miguel Mesa.

realities, allowing us to make certain territories visible and mobilise imagined geographies. We portrayed some practices of living heritage that deserve to be protected and, departing from them, we propose strategies of socio-spatial interventions that enable us to tell another story of Moravia to the city.[35]

Public engagement requires a pedagogical strategy to reach the lay public of the vicinity. To do so, we partnered with urban journalists – LA Network – and a digital community radio – La Cuarta Estación – to present the collective project around living heritage and created a sequence of thematic programs discussing the findings and proposals. Later, these programs became a series of podcasts[36] to be more easily disseminated as audio files. In addition, we developed a social media campaign to position the notion of living heritage and ask around the value of the neighbourhood as well as the key messages, the open events, and results. We used not only the traditional social media outlets but also WhatsApp as a widespread communication channel. To involve influential city-making actors, we organised a webinar and invited city councillors, local researchers, local officials, and international guests of multilateral organisations such as Global Platform Right to the City and Habitat United Nations. This space serves not only to provide thematic input to the participants but also to transform the public events into spaces of discussion and commitment to amplify the proposals proposed by the alliance.

Building on the learnings of the first year, we decided to focus the second year on creating a website and a couple of material mobile artefacts, the construction of which was led by COONVITE. The thematic emphasis was on the migratory movements that have taken place towards, into, and from the neighbourhood's territory. The website[37] displays the summary of the research-based design of spatial strategies the teams proposed. This time, we partner with a local youth collective interested in audio-visual creation – RedTina – to support the participants in shaping videos that portray relevant stories of the neighbourhood's characters, places, and practices. The storytelling of videos underpins the empirical evidence where the spatial strategies were grounded. In a simultaneous process of engagement across organisations and students, the core members of the cooperative COONVITE led a design and construction process of a three-dimensional artefact – called La Moravita[38] – intended to display the experiences of the collaboratively produced content during the OPE in the strategic public space as means to triggering interaction and exchange with the community member. These mobile artefacts were used in the launch of the website and displayed fanzines with a summary of the collective work. Subsequently, these devices have been used by some of the partner organisations to champion different initiatives with the inhabitants of the neighbourhood.

To conclude, I have argued that research-based design, trans-local learning alliances, and critical pedagogy are pivotal for framing urban design as a progressive co-creative process. I have shown how we have collectively shaped the pedagogical project of the Overseas Practice Engagement as an example of the "beautiful messiness of learning partnerships".[39] This chapter also has highlighted how the digital sphere has open opportunities for knowledge co-production about the urban and thinking different strategies to shape political incidence as part of a critical pedagogy around urban strategies. Nonetheless, the process was highly challenging as the online modality heightened the sensorial deprivation of a fully immersive learning process. A disembodied collaboration has fewer rewards on the collective celebration that often is key in these processes. In sum, I pose that to promote collective spatial imagination in pandemic times, we need an urban design based on the dialogue of multiple knowledges, intergenerational learning, and daily stories as key to moving towards spatial justice.

Bibliography

Alcaldia de Medellin. *Moravia: Memorias de un Puerto Urbano Medellin.* Proyecto de Memoria Cultural Barrio Moravia, 2005.

BUDD. "OPE Terms of Reference". London: Development Planning Unit, University College London, 2020.

Fauveaud, Gabriel and Esposito, Adele. "Beyond Official Heritage Agendas: The Third Space of Conservation Practices in Phnom Penh, Cambodia". *Urban Studies*, 58:12 (2020): 2473–2489. Accessed February 10, 2021, doi:10.1177/0042098020951325.

Freire, Paulo. *Pedagogy of the City*, trans. Donaldo Macedo. New York: Continuum, 1993.

Freire, Paulo. *Letters to Christina: Reflections on My Life and Work*. New York: Routledge, 1996.

Fung, Dilly. *A Connected Curriculum for Higher Education*. London: UCL Press, 2017.

Garrison, Randy. *E-learning in the 21st Century: A Framework for Research and Practice*. New York: Taylor & Francis, 2011.

Greiner, Clemens and Sakdapolrak, Patrick. "Translocality: Concepts, Applications and Emerging Research Perspectives". *Geography Compass*, 7:5 (2013): 373–384. Accessed February 10, 2020, doi:10.1111/gec3.12048.

Kress, Tricia. "Inside the 'Thick Wrapper' of Critical Pedagogy and Research". *International Journal of Qualitative Studies in Education*, 24:3 (2011): 263–271. Accessed January 10, 2020, doi:10.1080/09518398.2011.569768.

Lundy, Mark; Gottret, María Verónica and Ashby, Jacqueline A. "Learning Alliances: An Approach for Building Multi-Stakeholder Innovation Systems". *ILAC Brief* No. 8. Rome: Institutional Learning and Change ILAC Initiative, 2005.

Moreno-Leguizamon, Carlos et al. "Learning Alliance Methodology: Contributions and Challenges for Multicultural Planning in Health Service Provision: A Case Study in Kent, UK". *Planning Theory & Practice*, 1–18 (2015): 17. Accessed February 10, 2020, doi:10.1080/14649357.2014.990403

Ng, Mee Kam. "Knowledge and Power in Regenerating Lived Space in Treasure Hill, Taipei 1960s–2010: From Squatter Settlement to a Co-living Artist Village". *Planning Perspectives*, 30:2 (2014): 253–270. Accessed February 10, 2021, doi:10.1080/02665433.2014.934711

Ortiz, Catalina. "Ethics of Engagement in Design Research". In *BUDD Lab: Dwelling Practices in the City*. London: The Bartlett Development Planning Unit, UCL, 2017.

Ortiz, Catalina. *Comparative Urban Design: Exploring Border-making Practices in Medellin and Beirut*. Series: Cities, Design and Transformation, Volume 2. Development Planning Unit. London: UCL, 2018.

Ortiz, Catalina. "Medellin". In *Wiley-Blackwell Encyclopedia of Urban and Regional Studies*, ed. Anthony Orum. Wiley-Blackwell, 2019. Accessed January 10, 2020, doi:10.1002/9781118568446.eurs0194.

Ortiz, Catalina. "Prefacio". In: *Atlas de Patrimonio de Vivo de Moravia: una herramienta para pensar el futuro urbano*, ed. C. Ortiz and M. Yepes. Medellin: CDCM, The Bartlett Development Planning Unit – UCL Coonvite, Moravia Resiste, 2020.

Ortiz, Catalina and Hofmann, Pascal. *The DPU Online Teaching and Learning Strategy*. London: The Bartlett Development Planning Unit, University College London, 2020.

Patel, Kamna "Teaching and Learning in the Tropics: An Epistemic Exploration of "the Field" in a Development Studies Field Trip". *Journal of Geography in Higher Education*, 39:4 (2015) 584–594. Accessed February 10, 2020, doi:10.1080/03098265.2015.1084499.

Petrescu, Doina. "Learn to Act for an Engaged Everyday Life". In *LEARN TO ACT. Introducing the Eco-nomadic School*, ed. Kathrin Böhm, Tom James and Doina Petrescu, 316–320. Berlin: aaa/peprav Publishers, 2017.

Poulios, Ioannis. "Discussing Strategy in Heritage Conservation. Living Heritage Approach as an Example of Strategic Innovation". *Journal of Cultural Heritage, Management and Sustainable Development*, 4:1 (2014) 16–34.

Porter, Libby. "Partnerships of Learning for Planning Education, Who is Learning What from Whom? The Beautiful Messiness of Learning

Partnerships". *Planning Theory & Practice*, 16:3 (2015) 411. Accessed January 10, 2020, doi:10.1080/14649357.2015.1060688.

Siemens, George. "Connectivism: A Learning Theory for the Digital Age". *International Journal of Instructional Technology and Distance Learning*, 2(1) (2005): 3–10.

Sletto, Bjørn. "Educating Reflective Practitioners: Learning to Embrace the Unexpected through Service Learning". *Journal of Planning Education and Research*, 29(4) (2010): 403–415. Accessed February 10, 2020, doi:10.1177/0739456X10362771.

Sweet, Elizabeth, Sanders, Rickie and Peters, Donna-Marie. "Reversing the Gaze, Insiders Out, Outsiders In: Stories from the Ivory Tower and the Field". *Journal of Urban Affairs*, 43(2) (2019): 1–14. Accessed February 10, 2020, doi:10.1080/07352166.2019.1645570.

Notes

1 Dilly Fung, *A Connected Curriculum for Higher Education* (London: UCL Press, 2017): 165.
2 Catalina Ortiz and Pascal Hofmann, *The DPU Online Teaching and Learning Strategy* (London: The Bartlett Development Planning Unit, University College London, 2020).
3 Kamna Patel, "Teaching and Learning in the Tropics: An Epistemic Exploration of 'the Field' in a Development Studies Field Trip", *Journal of Geography in Higher Education*, 39:4 (2015) 584–594, accessed February 10, 2020, doi:10.1080/03098265.2015.1084499
4 Bjørn Sletto, "Educating Reflective Practitioners: Learning to Embrace the Unexpected through Service Learning", *Journal of Planning Education and Research*, 29:4 (2010) 413, accessed February 10, 2020, doi:10.1177/0739456X10362771.
5 Paulo Freire, *Pedagogy of the City*, trans. Donaldo Macedo (New York: Continuum, 1993): 77.
6 Freire, *Pedagogy of the City*, 74.
7 Freire, *Pedagogy of the City*, 77.
8 Paulo Freire, *Letters to Christina: Reflections on My Life and Work* (New York: Routledge, 1996): 113–114.
9 Tricia Kress, "Inside the 'Thick Wrapper' of Critical Pedagogy and Research", *International Journal of Qualitative Studies in Education*, 24:3 (2011) 263, accessed January 10, 2020, doi:10.1080/09518398.2011.569768
10 Freire, *Pedagogy of the City*, 132.
11 Catalina Ortiz, "Ethics of Engagement in Design Research", in *BUDD Lab: Dwelling Practices in the City* (London: The Bartlett Development Planning Unit, UCL, 2017): 11.
12 George Siemens "Connectivism: A Learning Theory for the Digital Age", *International Journal of Instructional Technology and Distance Learning*, 2:1 (2005) 3–10.
13 Randy Garrison, *E-learning in the 21st Century: A Framework for Research and Practice* (New York: Taylor & Francis, 2011) 184.

14 Catalina Ortiz, "Medellin", in *Wiley-Blackwell Encyclopedia of Urban and Regional Studies*. ed. Orum, Anthony (Wiley-Blackwell, 2019): 3, accessed January 10, 2020, doi: 10.1002/9781118568446.eurs0194
15 Ortiz, *Medellin*, 2.
16 BUDD, "OPE Terms of Reference" (London: Development Planning Unit, University College London, 2020): 45.
17 BUDD, OPE Terms of Reference, 4.
18 Elizabeth Sweet, Rickie Sanders and Donna-Marie Peters, "Reversing the Gaze, Insiders Out, Outsiders In: Stories from the Ivory Tower and the Field", *Journal of Urban Affairs*, 43:2 (2019) 1–14, accessed February 10, 2020, doi.org/10.1080/07352166.2019.1645570
19 Sletto, *Educating Reflective Practitioners: Learning to Embrace the Unexpected through Service Learning*, 405.
20 Mark Lundy, María Verónica Gottret, Jacqueline A. Ashby, "Learning Alliances: An Approach for Building Multi-stakeholder Innovation Systems". *ILAC Brief* No. 8 (Rome: Institutional Learning and Change ILAC Initiative, 2005): 25.
21 Carlos Moreno-Leguizamon, et al. "Learning Alliance Methodology: Contributions and Challenges for Multicultural Planning in Health Service Provision: A Case Study in Kent, UK", *Planning Theory & Practice*, 1–18 (2015): 17, accessed February 10, 2020, doi:10.1080/14649357.2014.990403
22 Moreno-Leguizamon, *Learning Alliance Methodology: Contributions and Challenges for Multicultural Planning in Health Service Provision: A Case Study in Kent*, UK, 16.
23 Catalina Ortiz, *Comparative Urban Design: Exploring border-making practices in Medellin and Beirut* (London: Series: Cities, Design and Transformation, Volume 2. Development Planning Unit, UCL, 2018): 236.
24 Clemens Greiner and Patrick Sakdapolrak, "Translocality: Concepts, Applications and Emerging Research Perspectives", *Geography Compass*, 7:5 (2013): 373–384, accessed February 10, 2020, doi:10.1111/gec3.12048
25 Greiner and Sakdapolrak, *Translocality: Concepts, Applications and Emerging Research Perspectives*, 380.
26 Ortiz, *Comparative Urban Design: Exploring border-making practices in Medellin and Beirut*, 236.
27 Catalina Ortiz, "Prefacio", in *Atlas de PatrimonioVivo*, ed. C. Ortiz and M. Yepes (Medellin: CDCM, The Bartlett Development Planning Unit – UCL Coonvite, Moravia Resiste, 2020): 155.
28 BUDD, *OPE Terms of Reference*, 8.
29 Gabriel Fauveaud and Adele Esposito, "Beyond Official Heritage Agendas: The Third Space of Conservation Practices in Phnom Penh, Cambodia", *Urban Studies*, 58:12 (2020) 2473–2489, accessed February 10, 2021, doi.org/10.1177/0042098020951325
30 Ioannis Poulios, "Discussing Strategy in Heritage Conservation. Living Heritage Approach as an Example of Strategic Innovation", *Journal of Cultural Heritage, Management and Sustainable Development*, 4:1 (2014) 16–34.
31 Mee Kam Ng, "Knowledge and Power in Regenerating Lived Space in Treasure Hill, Taipei 1960s–2010: From Squatter Settlement to a Co-living

Artist Village", *Planning Perspectives*, 30:2 (2014) 253–270, accessed February 10, 2021, doi: 10.1080/02665433.2014.934711
32 Poulios, *Discussing Strategy in Heritage Conservation. Living Heritage Approach as an example of Strategic Innovation*, 35.
33 Ortiz, *Ethics of Engagement in Design Research*, 11.
34 https://archive.org/details/atlas-patrimonio-vivo-moravia-futuro/mode/2up
35 Ortiz, Prefacio, 2.
36 https://centroculturalmoravia.org/moravia-living-heritage-atlas/
37 http://patrimoniovivo.centroculturalmoravia.site
38 https://patrimoniovivo.centroculturalmoravia.site/documentacion-documentation/
39 Porter, *Partnerships of Learning for Planning Education, Who is Learning What from Whom? The Beautiful Messiness of Learning Partnerships*, 412.

Index

Note: *Italic* page numbers refer to figures.

Acropoli 48
acupuncture 44
After the Planners (Goodman) 80
agency 3, 67, 79; of Integral Neighborhood Upgrading 106, 111
American architecture education, design-build teaching in 13
Anderson, Jane 13, 14
Applied Design program 34
A.R.C.A. 46
Archistart 48, 58–59
Architectural Association (AA) 14
architectural design service-learning 89–91, *91*; living lab as learning environment 92; relevance of reflective practice 92; service-learning participatory design 91
architectural education: experiential gap 21; problem-based learning of 21; professional knowledge gap 21; signature pedagogy of 22
"Artisan cheese factory and kindergarten" project 70, *70*
Atlas of Living Heritage 117, *117*
Autocostruzione Urbanismo Tattico (AUT) 43; student project experience 45–46, *47*; Tablo' project (*see* Tablo' project); team activities 46–48

Barcelona County Council 78
barrios populares 106
The Bartlett Development Planning Unit (DPU) 105, 107
Birmingham School of Architecture 13
Bloch, Noemi 45
British architectural education, pedagogical critique of live project 13
Brown, James Benedict 2, 4
Bruce, Bertram C. 45
Bruyneel, Geraldine 5
Building and Urban Design in Development (BUDD) 105, 109; fighting eviction threads *109,* 109–111
Building Beyond Borders symposium 18
Building Regulations of the City 51
bureaucracy 51

Camposaz 48
Catalan schools, Barcelona 63
change, actions towards 65–66
Citizen Designers 34
civic involvement 5, 58, 78
co-creation process 4, 85, *86,* 93, 94; SMH projects 86–87, *87*
co-designing temporary housing, on urban waiting spaces 98, 99
co-design phase, SMH project 88
co-development and dissemination phase, SMH project 89
COiNVITE 113
Collectif ETC 48
Col-Legno 48
Collettivo Orizzontale 52

community-based Early Childhood Development (ECD) centres 9
Community-engaged Architectural Design Learning (CEADL) 83, 84, 100
community-engaged learning 3
community participation 66–67
complexity 1, 66, 90, 98, 111
Cooman, Ken De 5
COONVITE 106, 113, 118
co-planning phase, SMH project 88
Corridò 56
COVID-19 pandemic 15, 16, 78; forced intermission of 17
critical approach 77–79
Critical Heritage Studies 114
critical pedagogy 2, 107–109, 113, 119
Critical Spatial Practice (CSP) 83, 84, 97–98; challenges and future directions 100; reflections on community-engaged architectural design learning as 98–99; SMH project, from reflective practice to 93–95
crossbenching 83; SMH project, from reflective practice to 93–95
Crysler, C. Greig 77
CSP *see* Critical Spatial Practice (CSP)
Culkin, John 18

decision-making process 12; to self-building 71–77, *72, 74, 76*
design-and-build workshop 46
design-build approach 2, 3; confusing 14–15; disentangling 12–14
design-build projects, lesson from advocates of 20
Design/Build Studio 9, 16
design-build teaching, in American architecture education 13
Design + Make 14
De Smet, Aurelie 5
Destination Moon 28
Dewey, John 2, 88
dialogic student-teacher interaction 2
Die Baupiloten Methods 68
diegetic prototype 27–29
diegetic prototyping 27, 29

digital co-design process: affective interactions in 114, *114*; ethics of engagement and care 116; phases of digital encounters 116–117; preparatory work and teams composition 115–116; research-based design framework 115
dislocation 17–18
distributed public engagement *117*, 117–119
Dunne, Anthony: *Speculative Everything: Design, Fiction, and Social Dreaming* 27
dwelling 32, *33,* 37, *38*
Dyke, Cameron Van 4

Education Africa 9
Ente Parco del Po Torinese 51
ethics of engagement, digital co-design process 116
experiential education 1–2
experiential gap, between architectural education and practice 21
experiential learning 2; original and hybrid forms of 3; principles of 21; service learning 83, 88
experiments: in construction 13–14; with primitive off-grid living 29; with social and experiential modes of design knowledge construction 1; through research and reworking of participative project methods 59

Fals-Borda, Orlando 68
Fattinger, Peter 45
Ferraris, Tommaso 5, 46
fossil fuels 26
"free building activity" 51
Freire, Paulo 2, 88, 107, 108
Fuller, R. Buckminster 27
funding program 46
Future Cycles project *28,* 29, 35

Gerbino, Carlotta 5, 46
Global Platform Right to the City 118
Goodman, Robert: *After the Planners* 80
green energy 26

Index

green technology 26
Greiner, Clemens 112

Habitat United Nations 118
Heben, Andrew: *Tent City Urbanism: From Self-Organized Camps to Tiny House Villages* 34
Hirst, Paul 80
Hohenbüchler, Christine 66
Holub, Barbara 66
Hooke Park 14–15
humanity 25

il Valentino 51
Imbarchino del Valentino 49–50, 52, 53, 55
impact: of built projects on-site 78; of digital tools on learning 107; student 37, *38,* 39
industrialization 26
informal community 114
informal settlements 106
innovation/innovative 10, 26, 45, 46, 49, 59, 112; of architectural education 1; educational practice 58; in urban governance 110
Integral Neighborhood Upgrading 106
international-related experiences 64
involvement 48; civic 5, 58, 78
Irish architectural education, pedagogical critique of live project 13

Jones, Douglas 14

Kirby, David 27–28, 35
Kraus, Chad 13, 14, 20

La Cuarta Estación 118
La Moravita 118
LA Network 118
LaSTIn 53
Latour, Bruno 67
Lavelle, Louis 67
learning alliance approach 111
learning by doing approach 44, 45
Leeds Beckett University 15
Lefebvre, H. 77
Lewin, Kurt 68

liquidity 1
live-build 21–22
live project approach 2, 3, 92–93
live projects: confusing 14–15; disentangling 12–14; pedagogical critique of 13
living lab, as learning environment 92
Llonch, Roger-Joan Sauquet 5

Mas Vilanova built project 71–73, *72*
Medellin model 110
Medieval old town of Cardona 75–77, *76*
Micro Ecovillage Project: context of 29–31; development of 31–33; goals of 35; inspiration and precedence 34–35; purpose of 35–36; structure of 33–34; student impact 37, *38,* 39; teaching and learning opportunities 36–37
Miessen, Markus 94, 97, 98
Montacchini, Elena 5
Moore, Charles 13
Moravia Cultural Centre (CDCM) 113
Moravia Cultural Development Centre 106
Moravia Resiste 106, *109,* 113
Moreno-Leguizamon, Carlos 112
multiplicity 1, 106, 110

non-governmental organisations (NGOs) 9

Oasis river park project 73–75, *74*
online learning community 107
open process 65–66
Opportunity Village, in Eugene 35
Orbit *28,* 29
Orizzontale 50–51
Overseas Practice Engagement (OPE) 105–107, 109, 119; fighting eviction threads *109,* 109–111

Pak, Burak 5
Pallasmaa, Juhani: *The Thinking Hand* 71
Parco del Valentino 49, 55
Partial Plan of Integral Improvement of Moravia 110

Index

participation 48; of AUT, in City of Turin 49; in and through design, SMH project 95–96, *96*
participatory action research (PAR) 68, 84, *85*
participatory design workshop, between students and citizens 68–69, *69*
The Participatory Mind (Skolimowski) 71
pedagogical discourse 13
pedagogical space, design studio 15
pedagogy of experience 112
physical experimentation 71–77, *72, 74, 76*
physical space, design studio 15
Politecnico di Torino 46, 49
Politecnico funding program 46
positive replacement 27
Poulios, Ioannis 115
poverty 16
Priest, Colin 13, 14
problem-based learning, of architectural education 21
production-as-research 97
professionalizing workshops 48
professional knowledge gap, between architectural education and practice 21
Project Jouberton, Klerksdorp 10, *10*
Project Lesedi, Limpopo Province *19*
Project Mothopong, Limpopo Province *19*
"protected reality" 46
public engagement 118
public imagination 26–27; Micro Ecovillage Project (*see* Micro Ecovillage Project); Orbit *28, 29*
The Public Realm (Sennett) 66
public space 65; transformation of 49

Raby, Fiona: *Speculative Everything: Design, Fiction, and Social Dreaming* 27
Recyclo 48
RedTina 118
reflecting-on-action 94
reflection-in-action 94
reflective practice 92; to CSP and crossbenching, SMH project 93–95

Rendell, Jane 97, 98
research-based design 108; framework, digital co-design process 115; of spatial strategies 118; trans-local learning alliances for 111–114
research-driven service-learning 88
resilience 78, 84
restraint 26
Rhodes Must Fall campaign 16
Rural Studio of Auburn University 34, 45
Russell, Peter 2, 4

Sakdapolrak, Patrick 112
salt 75
Sara, Rachel 13
schools of architecture 15, 20, 22, 43, 49, 63, 77
Schoonjans, Yves 5
self-built construction 71
self-construction workshops 47, 48, 52
self-led group of students 46
Sennett, Richard 65; *The Public Realm* 66
Serra-Permanyer, Marta 5
service-learning 65, 83; course 89; participatory design 91; pedagogy 107
Service-Learning Agreement 65
Shaw, Bernard 12
Skolimowski, Henryk: *The Participatory Mind* 71
slum upgrading 106, 111
SMH CEADL approach 98
SMH Model (SMH/M) 86, *87*
social return 66–71, *69, 70*
Social Urbanism 110
society: industrialized 27; modern 26; social function in 64; space 77
socio-cultural space, design studio 15
Solar Decathlon competitions 64
solar photovoltaic system 32, *32*
Solidary Mobile Housing (SMH) research project 83; action research cycles 85; co-creation model integrated with architectural design service learning 86–87, *87*; impressions of co-creation

process 85, *86*; live project approach as specific type of living lab 92–93; participants in 84; participatory action research 84, *85*; from participatory design to participation in and through design 95–96, *96*; from reflective practice to CSP and crossbenching 93–95; research questions of 84; teaching and learning embedded in 88–89
Soprintendenza Archeologia Belle Arti e Paesaggio 51
spatial injustice 1, 105
Speculative Everything: Design, Fiction, and Social Dreaming (Dunne and Raby) 27
student activism 46
studio-based pedagogy 109
summer events 49
"Supershed and Pods" concept 34
sustainability, problem with 26
sustainable technology 26
Sustainable Technology students 32, *32*
Sweet, Elizabeth 111

Tablo' project 48; construction phase 52–55, *53, 54*; context and municipality call 49–50; design phase 50–52; use and aftermath 55–56, *56, 57*
tactical urbanism 43
Teaching-Learning-Research: Design and Environments 18
Tedesco, Silvia 5
temporal space, design studio 15
temporary spaces 43
temporary tactical action 43–45; experience of 59
Tent City Urbanism: From Self-Organized Camps to Tiny House Villages (Heben) 34

The Thinking Hand (Pallasmaa) 71
Thušanang Trust 9, 20–21
Till, Jeremy 99
Transducers: Collective Pedagogies and Spatial Politics (Collados and Rodrigo) 68
transformative participation 65
trans-locality 112
trans-local learning alliances, for research-based design 111–114
Turtle Island Preserve 29, *30*
Twain, Mark 18

UHasselt 18
uncertainty, actions towards 65–66
University of Nottingham (UoN) 9
University of Sheffield 15, 20
unsustainable energy sources 26
UoN Design/Build Studio 14, 20; COVID-19 16; history of 10–12; international travel 17
urban interventions 109, 110, 117
urbanism, defined as 44
urban regeneration 43

Vallès School of Architecture (ETSAV) 64, 79–80; critical approach 77–79; open process 65–66; pedagogical objective 64–65; physical experimentation 71–77, *72, 74, 76*; social return 66–71, *69, 70*
Van Heesvelde, Tineke 5
Vantournhout, Sara 5

wood storage racks *31, 32*
World Expositions 49

Yale School of Architecture 13
Young Talent Architecture Award 75

zones of conflict 99

For Product Safety Concerns and Information please contact our EU representative GPSR@taylorandfrancis.com
Taylor & Francis Verlag GmbH, Kaufingerstraße 24, 80331 München, Germany

www.ingramcontent.com/pod-product-compliance
Lightning Source LLC
Chambersburg PA
CBHW051751230426
43670CB00012B/2243